SAINT ANTHONY
OF PADUA

His Life, Legends,
and Devotions

· · · · · · · · · · · · · · · · · · ·

EDITED BY JACK WINTZ, O.F.M.

ST. ANTHONY MESSENGER PRESS
Cincinnati, Ohio

Cover and book design by Mark Sullivan
Cover image:
St. Anthony of Padua (tempera on panel)
by Bartolomeo Vivarini (1432-99)
Musee des Beaux-Arts, Tours, France/ Giraudon/
The Bridgeman Art Library

LIBRARY OF CONGRESS CATALOGING-IN-PUBLICATION DATA
Anthony of Padua : his life, legends, and devotions / edited by Jack Wintz.
p. cm.
Rev. ed. of: Anthony of Padua, saint of the people.
ISBN 978-1-61636-324-6 (alk. paper)
1. Anthony, of Padua, Saint, 1195-1231. 2. Christian saints—Italy—Biography.
I. Wintz, Jack. II. Anthony of Padua, saint of the people.
BX4700.A6A587 2012
282.092—dc23
[B]
2012003317

ISBN 978-1-61636-324-6

Published by St. Anthony Messenger Press
28 W. Liberty St.
Cincinnati, OH 45202
www.AmericanCatholic.org
www.SAMPBooks.org

Printed in the U.S.A.
Printed on acid-free paper.

12 13 14 15 16   5 4 3 2 1

CONTENTS

FOREWORD

This book has been revised, and is a rather extensive expansion of the original popular little book *Saint Anthony of Padua: The Story of his Life and Popular Devotions*. The original, published in 1993, was built essentially around two articles that appeared in the June 1992 issue of *St. Anthony Messenger* magazine. That issue marked the start of the one hundredth anniversary celebration of *St. Anthony Messenger*, the national magazine whose first issue was published by the Franciscan Friars of Cincinnati in June 1893. In 2005 the book was rereleased with several more chapters that also came from previously published *St. Anthony Messenger* magazine articles. And in this edition three new chapters appear.

The original articles that were published in 1992 were written by veteran writers and well-loved friars who have since passed on to their Maker. Both friars were former editors of *St. Anthony Messenger*. The first article, by Leonard Foley, O.F.M., which dealt chiefly with the life and legends of St. Anthony, has been updated a little bit and is now spread out over the first two chapters of the book you hold in your hands. It originally bore the title "Finding the Real St. Anthony." The article "Finder, Teacher, Matchmaker, Guide: Devotions to St. Anthony," written by Fr. Norman Perry, O.F.M., describes the various customs, titles, and devotions that became closely associated with Anthony over the centuries. That chapter, which was also adapted, is chapter nine of the present book.

This new edition includes three new chapters that give further details and more in-depth explanations of Anthony's travels and retreats. I wrote the articles, which originally appeared in *St. Anthony Messenger*.

In the new chapter two we visit St. Anthony's birthplace in a niche below the church that bears his name and marks the place where he was born. Then, we come to the Lisbon Cathedral where Anthony was baptized before stopping at the monastery where he prepared to become an Augustinian monk. Finally, we travel a hundred miles north to where Anthony was ordained an Augustinian priest. Then, somewhat surprisingly, he joins the Franciscans and sails to Morocco to preach the gospel to the Muslims.

In chapter three we learn how Anthony left Morocco and ended up in Italy, where attended the Franciscan chapter of Pentecost (1221) near Assisi and took an assignment in northern Italy. There he lived in a Franciscan hermitage until an ordination ceremony in Forlí, Italy, catapulted him into a new career, as theologian and itinerant preacher, that ended with his death near Padua.

Finally, in the new chapter eight we visit five places where St. Anthony sought contemplative union with God. The places are the hermitage of Monte Paolo, a grotto above Spoleto, le Celle di Cortona, a cave at Mount La Verna, and a tree hut near Padua.

Those who feel especially drawn to Anthony as spiritual guide, friend, and intercessor—and who have a special fondness for the novena form of prayer—may find chapter twelve, "Making a Novena to St. Anthony," particularly appealing. The chapter includes an actual nine-day novena designed to help the faithful find a deeper relationship with God through Anthony's guidance and intercession. This new novena contains not only several traditional prayers already familiar to many readers but also nine short passages from sermons of Anthony, which will help lead to the presence of God. Each of the nine sermon passages—one for each day of the novena—is accompanied by a brief daily reflection, newly written for this edition of the book.

You don't have to read this book from beginning to end. If Anthony's life story intrigues you, simply begin with part one. If you are more interested in his legends, go directly to part two. Does his contemplative life and practices intrigue you? Go directly to part three. Whether you have a lifelong love of and devotion to Anthony and desire to know more, or you only know to pray to him when your keys are lost, you will find something new to love about him in this little collection about a larger-than-life saint.

Jack Wintz, O.F.M.
January 2012

Introducing St. Anthony

A favorite in much of the Catholic world, St. Anthony of Padua has more cities and places named after him than any other saint—sixty-eight. This includes forty-four in Latin America, fifteen in the United States, four in Canada, four in the Philippines, and one in Spain. Four capes, three bays, two reefs, and two peaks also take his name.

Even more numerous have been, until recently, the statues of St. Anthony in churches, where he is depicted holding the Christ child, the book of Scriptures, and a lily or a flaming torch.

A Saint with a Worldwide Appeal

Obviously Anthony must have been a favorite of missionaries who took this likeable saint to the Western Hemisphere and to many other lands around the world. But over the years it seems to have been laypeople who have adopted St. Anthony of Padua as a kind of all-purpose saint—finder of lost articles, helper in troubles, healer of bodies and spirits. Hundreds of thousands have prayed the quaint old responsory: "If miracles thou fain would see, Lo, error, death, calamity…"

We might be tempted to ask, as a friar once asked St. Francis of Assisi, "Why after you? Why after you?" The answer seems to be both the immense popularity of St. Anthony in his lifetime and the flood of wonders that followed his death.

In *St. Anthony: Doctor of the Church*, Franciscan scholar Sophronius Clasen, O.F.M., wrote:

> Immediately after his death, Anthony became the object of an extraordinary devotion; and miracle followed miracle, as the prayers of the sick and afflicted were answered by sudden cures and other wonders. This set on foot a great wave of enthusiasm, and drew large crowds to his tomb, who began to honor him as a Saint even before the Pope had canonized him. Often orderly processions were formed; and these were led sometimes by the bishop of Padua and his clergy. The leading knights of the city and the students of the university all took part; and all carried candles of great size.

FINDING THE REAL ST. ANTHONY

Older, unremodeled churches almost always count St. Anthony among their collection of statues. The saint of Padua is usually sculpted or portrayed holding in his arms the child Jesus, a lily, a book, or all three. A bank of vigil lights will burn in front of the statue.

Tuesday evening is the traditional time of St. Anthony novena devotions, with prayers to St. Anthony, benediction, and the reading of petitions written on little scraps of paper: "for a safe delivery," "to obtain a job," "for reconciliation with my daughter," and, invariably, "to find my lost _____." On the saint's feast day, June 13, St. Anthony bread is blessed. And since the saint is the special patron of Italy, an honor he shares with St. Francis, many Italian families have a son named Anthony.

The list of human concerns for which Anthony is the patron is amazingly varied. Fr. Lothar Hardick, O.F.M., who wrote a book on the saint, tells us that St. Anthony has been known as the patron of lovers and of marriage, as a helper in time of birth or as a help against infertility. He was called upon against fevers, against diabolic powers, and against plagues among cattle. He was honored as the patron of mariners as well as of those who live in mountainous areas.

The array of wonders attributed to Anthony in story and legend is equally astounding in its variety. He was in two places at the same time; after a dare by an unbeliever and at Anthony's prayer, a donkey knelt before the Blessed Sacrament; fishes lifted their heads above the water to listen as he preached to them, after bored believers turned away; a foot severed by an ax was rejoined to its leg. Are these legends true or false? We will deal with this question later. But to get a reliable and factual summary of St. Anthony's life story, we go immediately to chapter one.

PART ONE

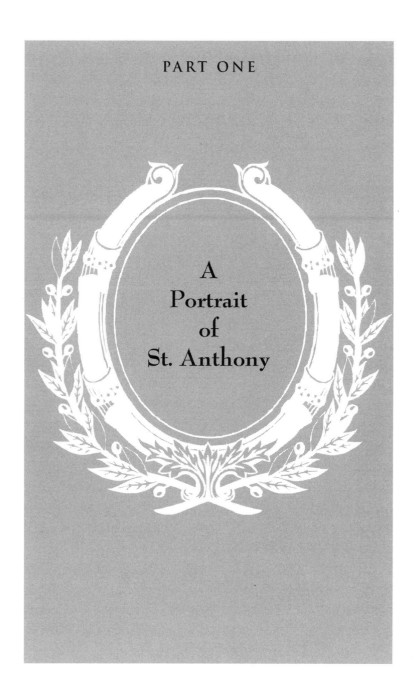

A
Portrait
of
St. Anthony

CHAPTER ONE

A Short Life of St. Anthony of Padua*
by Leonard Foley, O.F.M.

Anthony was born in 1195 (thirteen years after St. Francis) in Lisbon, Portugal, at the mouth of the Tagus River, from which explorers would later sail across the Atlantic. His parents, Martin and Mary Bulhom, belonged to one of the prominent families of the city and were among those who had been loyal in service to the king. The infant was baptized in the nearby cathedral at the foot of Castelo Sao Jorge, which still dominates the city. His parents named him Fernando. Fernando Bulhom attended the cathedral school and at the surprisingly young age of fifteen entered the religious order of St. Augustine. "Whoever enters a monastery," he later wrote, "goes, so to speak, to his grave." For Fernando, however, the monastery was far from peaceful, because his old friends came to visit so frequently. Their vehement political discussions hardly provided an atmosphere for prayer and study.

After two years of this, the young man asked to move and was sent to Coimbra, one hundred miles north. This was the beginning of nine years of intense study, including learning the Augustinian theology that he would later combine with the Franciscan vision. Fernando was ordained a priest probably during this time.

---

*Sophronius Clasen, O.F.M., has written an excellent biography of St. Anthony, *St. Anthony: Doctor of the Church.* This summary is based on that source.

ANTHONY JOINS THE FRANCISCANS

The life of this young priest took a crucial turn when the bodies of the first five Franciscan martyrs were returned from Morocco. These holy men had preached in the mosque in Seville, almost being martyred at the outset, but the sultan allowed them to pass on to Morocco, where, after continuing to preach Christ despite repeated warnings, they were tortured and beheaded. Now, in the presence of the queen and a huge crowd, their remains were carried in solemn procession to Fernando's monastery.

Overjoyed and inspired by the martyrs' heroic deaths, Fernando came to a momentous decision. He went to the little friary the queen had given the Franciscans in Coimbra and said, "Brother, I would gladly put on the habit of your Order if you would promise to send me as soon as possible to the land of the Saracens, that I may gain the crown of the holy martyrs." After some challenges from the prior of the Augustinians, he was allowed to leave that priory and receive the Franciscan habit, taking the name Anthony, after the patron of their local church and friary, St. Anthony of the Olives. He was allowed to take vows immediately, as the Order did not yet require a novitiate.

True to their promise, the friars allowed Anthony to go to Morocco, to be a witness for Christ and possibly a martyr as well. But, as often happens, the gift he wanted to give was not the gift that was to be asked of him. Anthony became seriously ill, and after several months he realized he had to go home.

DETOUR TO ITALY

He never did arrive home. His ship ran into storms and high winds and was blown east across the Mediterranean. Months later, he arrived on the east coast of Sicily. The friars at nearby Messina, though they didn't know him, welcomed him and began nursing him back to health. Still ailing, he wanted to attend the great chapter of the Pentecost Mats (so called because the three thousand friars could not be housed and slept on mats). Francis was there, also sick; however, history does not reveal any meeting between Francis and Anthony. Since Anthony was from "out of town," he received no assignment at the meeting, so he asked to go with a provincial superior from northern Italy. "Instruct me in the Franciscan life," he asked, not mentioning his prior theological training. Now, like Francis, he had his first choice—a life of seclusion and contemplation in a little hermitage near Monte Paolo.

Perhaps we would never have heard of Anthony if he hadn't gone to an ordination of Dominicans and Franciscans in 1222. As they gathered for a meal afterward, the provincial suggested that one of the friars give a short sermon. Quite typically, everybody respectfully declined. So Anthony was asked to give "just something simple," since he presumably had no education.

Anthony also demurred but finally began to speak in a simple, artless way. Suddenly, the fire within him became evident. His knowledge was unmistakable, but his holiness was what really impressed everyone there.

ANTHONY TURNS TO PREACHING

Now he was exposed. His quiet life of prayer and penance at the hermitage was exchanged for that of a public preacher. Francis heard of Anthony's previously hidden gifts, and Anthony was assigned to preach in northern Italy. It was not like preaching around Assisi, where the faith was strong: Here he ran into heretics, well organized and ardent.

The problem with many preachers in Anthony's day was that their lifestyles contrasted sharply with that of the poor people to whom they preached. In our experience, it could be compared to an evangelist arriving in a slum and driving a Mercedes, delivering a homily from his car and speeding off to a vacation resort.

The heresy of that time thus had its grain of truth. The so-called "Pure" (Cathari) began by wanting to go back to gospel poverty. Scandalized by the wealth of the Church, they practiced strict poverty and engaged in manual labor. But they also denied the validity of the hierarchy and the sacraments. They saw themselves as the only "real" Christians.

Anthony saw that words were obviously not enough. He had to *show* the Cathari gospel poverty. People wanted more than self-disciplined, even penitent, priests. They wanted the unselfish genuineness of gospel living. And in Anthony they found it. They were moved by who he was more than by what he said. In Rimini, one hotbed of heresy, he was able to call the people together—that alone was a sign of his fame.

Despite his efforts, not everyone listened. Legend has it that one day, while preaching to deaf ears, Anthony went to the river and preached to the fishes. That, says the traditional tale, got *everyone's* attention.

Anthony traveled tirelessly in both northern Italy and southern France—perhaps four hundred trips—choosing to enter the cities where the heretics were strongest. Yet the sermons he has left behind rarely show him taking direct issue with the heretics. As the historian Clasen interprets it, Anthony preferred to present the grandeur of Christianity in positive ways. It was no good to prove people *wrong*. Anthony wanted to win them to the *right*, the healthiness of real sorrow and conversion, the wonder of reconciliation with a loving Father. The word *fire* recurs in descriptions of him. And though he was called the "Hammer of Heretics," the word *warmth* describes him more fully.

Public Preacher, Franciscan Teacher

Anthony's superior, St. Francis, was cautious about education such as his protégé possessed. He had seen too many theologians taking pride in their sophisticated knowledge. Still, if the friars had to hit the road and preach to all sorts of people, they needed a firm grounding in Scripture and theology. So, when he heard the glowing report of Anthony's debut at the ordination, Francis wrote in 1224, "It pleases me that you should teach the friars sacred theology, provided that in such studies they do not destroy the spirit of holy prayer and devotedness, as contained in the Rule."

Anthony first taught in a friary in Bologna, which became a famous school. The theology book of the time was the Bible. In one of Anthony's extant sermons, there are at least one hundred and eighty-three passages from Scripture. While none of his theological conferences and discussions were written down, we do have two volumes of his sermons: *Sunday Sermons* and *Feastday Sermons*. His method included much allegory and symbolical explanation of Scripture. Nature was a fertile field from which Anthony gathered symbols and allegories—as did Jesus—such as the lilies of the field, the nest of birds, the web of the spider, the last cry of the dying swan. But above all, Anthony made references to *fire*, which is why he is sometimes portrayed with a book (the Bible) in one hand and, with the other, holding a flame out toward the onlooker.

On the occasion of St. Anthony being declared a doctor of the Church (January 16, 1946), the minister general of the Friars Minor, Valentine Schaaf, wrote:

> Our Holy Doctor was the connecting link which joined the chain of the ancient Augustinian tradition [which Anthony had learned in Coimbra] to the then barely emerging Franciscan school.... After Anthony it was especially the Seraphic Doctor Saint Bonaventure and the Venerable John Duns Scotus, the Subtle Doctor, who continued to adhere more rigidly and faithfully to the Augustinian spirit, which is briefly expressed in the following words: "The fulfillment

and the end of the Law and of all divine Scriptures is love."
Both unanimously assert that theology is a practical science
insofar as it is the end of theology to move and lead man to
love God.

Anthony continued to preach as he taught the friars and assumed
more responsibility within the Order. In 1226 he was appointed
provincial superior of northern Italy, but he still found time for
contemplative prayer in a small hermitage. Around Easter in 1228
(he was only thirty-three years old), he went to Rome, where he
met Pope Gregory IX, who had been a faithful friend of and adviser
to St. Francis. Naturally, the famous preacher was invited to speak.
He did it humbly, as always. The response was so great that to many
people it seemed that the miracle of Pentecost was repeated.

PADUA ENTERS THE PICTURE

Padua, Italy, is a short distance west of Venice. At the time of Anthony,
it was one of the most important cities in the country, with a university for the study of civil and canon law. Religion there was at a low
point. There was constant fighting between the tyrant Ezzelino, a
ruthless, brutal man who led the Ghibellines, and the Guelph party
in nearby Verona. Anthony divided his time between solitude, to
write the two volumes of his sermons, and preaching to the people
of Padua. Sometimes he left Padua for greater solitude. He went to
a place loved by Francis—Mount La Verna, where Francis received
the wounds of Jesus. He also found a grotto near the friary where
he could pray in silence and solitude.

In poor health and still serving as provincial superior of northern
Italy, he went to the general chapter in Rome and asked to be
relieved of his duties. But he was later recalled as part of a special
commission to discuss certain matters of the Franciscan Rule with
the pope.

Back in Padua, he preached his last and most famous lenten sermons. The crowds were so great—sometimes thirty thousand—that the churches could not hold them, so he went into the piazzas or the open fields. People waited all night to hear him. He needed a bodyguard to protect him from the people armed with scissors who wanted to cut off a piece of his habit as a relic. After his morning Mass and sermon, he would hear confessions. This sometimes lasted all day—as did his fasting.

Anthony was instrumental in a matter of social justice. Under the law, a Paduan debtor was put in prison if he could not pay. A new law read: "At the request of the venerable Friar (and holy confessor) Anthony of the Order of Friars Minor, it is established and ordained that henceforth no one is to be held in prison for pecuniary debt." Debtors did have to relinquish their possessions, but they were free. In another instance of civic involvement, he failed to move the tyrant Ezzelino to release the leader of those opposing him. Anthony was so disappointed over this that he withdrew from public life.

ANTHONY'S LAST DAYS AND CANONIZATION

The great energy he had expended during Lent left him exhausted. He went to a little town near Padua, but seeing death coming close, he wanted to return to the city that he loved. "If it seems good to you," he said to one of the friars, "I should like to return to Padua to the friary of Santa Maria, so as not to be a burden to the friars here." The journey in a wagon weakened him so much, however, that he had to stop at Arcella. He had to bless Padua from a distance, as Francis had blessed Assisi.

At Arcella, Anthony received the last sacraments and sang and prayed with the friars there. When one of them asked Anthony what he was staring at so intently, he answered, "I see my Lord!" He died in peace a short time after that. He was only thirty-six and had been a Franciscan but ten years.

The following year, his friend Pope Gregory IX, moved by the many miracles that occurred at Anthony's tomb, declared him a saint. Many years later, during exhumation of Anthony's body for transferral, Anthony's tongue was found to be still lifelike and of a natural color, though the rest of his body had disintegrated. St. Bonaventure, head of all Franciscans in the world, was present at the transfer, and he cried out, "O blessed tongue, you have always praised the Lord and led others to praise him! Now we can clearly see how great indeed have been your merits before God!"

Anthony was a simple and humble friar who preached the Good News lovingly and with fearless courage. The youth whom his fellow friars thought was uneducated became one of the great preachers and theologians of his day. He was a man of great penance and apostolic zeal. But he was primarily a saint of the people.

CHAPTER TWO

The Portugal Years

by Jack Wintz, O.F.M.

To the people of Portugal, the saint that most of the world calls "Anthony of Padua" is better known as "Anthony of Lisbon." If we accept 1195 as his date of birth, as most historians do, this means that Anthony spent about twenty-five years of his life in Portugal, compared to only ten or eleven in Italy. No wonder the people of Portugal claim Anthony as their saint—even if he spent his later years in Italy, and died near Padua on June 13, 1231.

During four days in Portugal in the spring of 2010, our pilgrimage group focused its attention on four key shrines.

HIS BIRTHPLACE

Our first stop in Lisbon was at Anthony's place of birth. Anthony, whose original name was Fernando Bulhom, was born into a noble and influential family. His home stood only a block away from the Lisbon cathedral.

Fernando's birthplace is still an important pilgrimage destination in Lisbon. Thousands of pilgrims from around the world visit the saint's birthplace each month in a niche below the Church of Santo António. One of the shrine's most famous visitors in recent decades was Pope John Paul II, who made a stop there on May 12, 1982, on his way to Fatima.

Our group of pilgrims was able to celebrate Eucharist in this church and afterward climb down the stairs in small groups to visit the little niche marking the place where Fernando, the future Anthony, was born.

Lisbon Cathedral, Where He Was Baptized

Our next stop was Lisbon's twelfth-century cathedral, which stands only a block up the street from Fernando's birthplace. Here we gazed at the same font where he was baptized and which is still used today. Because his parents were devout Catholics and people of means, Fernando was able to attend the cathedral school and receive a fine Christian education from the priests who taught there.

We strolled through part of the district known as the Alfama, the neighborhood that surrounded Fernando's home. In his day, the Alfama was Lisbon's most attractive neighborhood. And its twisting maze of narrow and hilly streets, open patios, taverns, and restaurants is still appealing to tourists today.

If Fernando ever hiked to the top of the hills high above his home, and he probably did, he would eventually reach the Castelo de São Jorge (Castle of St. George). This became the residence of the earliest Portuguese royalty after it was regained from the Moors. Tourists visiting this castle and historic surroundings today can enjoy a magnificent view of the Tagus River, from which the Portuguese mariners of long ago sailed out to the farthest corners of the world.

Augustinian Monastery of St. Vincent

On the outskirts of Lisbon in Fernando's day, but not too far from his birthplace, stood the Monastery of St. Vincent. In 1210, at age fifteen, Fernando made the dramatic decision to leave home and enter this monastery of the Augustinians.

Our pilgrimage in Lisbon included a visit to the Church of St.

Vincent. The building that we entered and briefly toured was not the same building that Fernando knew. But the large structure still bears the name of St. Vincent and was rebuilt over the same location where as an aspiring friar Fernando had searched for God.

After spending two years at St. Vincent, he asked his prior if he could be transferred to another monastery where he might find a better climate for prayer and contemplation. Fernando believed his search for God was being compromised in Lisbon because old chums kept trying to visit him there. He requested to be transferred to the Augustinian monastery of Santa Cruz (Holy Cross) in the city of Coimbra. There he hoped to encounter a greater spirit of tranquility and fewer distractions.

MONASTERY OF SANTA CRUZ

When Fernando arrived in Coimbra, a hundred miles north of Lisbon, and entered this well-known monastery, he was really entering the most important cultural center in all of Portugal. Coimbra was then Portugal's capital city. Santa Cruz, with its well-stocked library and excellent teachers, was a center of Christian learning that could compete with the great Augustinian monasteries of France.

Historians believe that Fernando lived at Santa Cruz for about eight years. The young Augustinian friar advanced in his understanding of theology and the spiritual life. Here he absorbed the sacred Scriptures that became the heart of the sermons he preached as a Franciscan. It is commonly believed that Fernando was ordained an Augustinian priest in this church.

Santa Cruz has been rebuilt more than once over the centuries. Yet our group of pilgrims was still able to tour parts of the original monastery that Fernando would have known. Among these were the sacristy, the chapter room, the monastery gardens, and the arched corridors that border the gardens.

In 1220, Ferdinand's life took a surprising turn. It happened that the relics of five Franciscan martyrs, who had been beheaded earlier that year in Morocco for preaching the gospel to the Muslims, were carried into Coimbra amid great publicity and fervor. In fact, the relics ended up in the Monastery of Santa Cruz, where they have been safely kept and held in high esteem. They are still venerated there. Our group had a chance to see them during our visit and to reflect on their effect upon the life of St. Anthony. Today, the relics are stored inside two small silvery busts of Franciscan friars. They are on public display in a small niche at the end of a corridor off the sacristy.

Fernando, too, pondered the great faith and heroism of these Franciscan martyrs. He was twenty-five years of age. A strong desire grew within him to follow in their footsteps, to go to Morocco himself and become a martyr for Christ.

He would soon have a chance to act on this desire. One of Fernando's responsibilities at Santa Cruz was that of showing hospitality to visitors who came to the monastery's front door. A group of Franciscan friars, who lived at the nearby Church of St. Anthony, often showed up at the monastery door to ask for alms. On one occasion, Anthony spoke earnestly to them about his desire to become a Franciscan friar so that he, too, could be sent to Morocco to become a martyr for Christ.

The Franciscan friars assured him that this was possible and—to make a long story short—Fernando, the Augustinian, became Anthony, the Franciscan. He took his new name from the little church where the friars stayed and where he himself would stay for a time—a church named after St. Anthony of the Desert. Before long, Anthony set sail for Morocco—never to return to his beloved Portugal.

Anthony's formative years in Portugal were extremely important for this courageous native son. Very likely, he would have never become a great teacher and evangelist—or saintly friar and doctor of the Church—had it not been for the opportunities of education, religious training, and profound spiritual growth that shaped his early life in Portugal, the land of his birth.

CHAPTER THREE

The Italy Years
by Jack Wintz, O.F.M.

To Anthony's deep disappointment, his mission to become a martyr for Christ in Morocco failed. Anthony fell seriously ill there and set sail back for Portugal in hope of regaining his health, or so he thought. But on the journey back, a mighty wind swept the ship badly off course and it landed in Sicily.

ANTHONY GOES TO ASSISI, MONTE PAOLO, AND FORLÌ

With fraternal care, the friars in Sicily nursed Anthony back to reasonably good health and encouraged him to go along with them to the Franciscan chapter of Pentecost near Assisi, in central Italy.

St. Francis of Assisi, the order's founder, was there. Anthony certainly saw or heard Francis and may have met him on this occasion.

Because Anthony was a newcomer to the order, the chapter ended without his receiving any formal assignment. So Anthony took the initiative to introduce himself to the provincial minister of the Romagna region in northern Italy and asked to travel back with him and stay in one of the friaries of his province.

Because Anthony was still recuperating from his illness and perhaps, too, from the emotional disappointment of his failed mission in Morocco, he was longing for a place of prayer and tranquility to sort out his life in a new land.

In Romagna, Anthony discovered just that kind of opportunity. The provincial asked him to serve as priest for four brothers living in a hermitage at Monte Paolo, not far from the town of Forlì. He would have plenty of time for solitary prayer. Anthony learned, moreover, that one of the friars at the hermitage had built a cell in a cave nearby that would be ideal for this kind of prayer. With the friar's approval, Anthony went out from the hermitage almost every day to pray in the cave and reinforce his union with God. For penance, he took with him only some bread and a small container of water. Anthony lived at the hermitage of Monte Paolo for nearly eleven months.

Then came an event that would change Anthony's life forever. He and the other friars were invited to an ordination ceremony in the town of Forlì, located some ten miles from Monte Paolo. A good number of Franciscan and Dominican friars were there. The local superior invited several Dominicans to address those assembled, but all begged off. Finally, the superior turned to Anthony and insisted that he share with the invited guests whatever the Holy Spirit might inspire him to say.

Anthony complied with the superior's wishes and preached humbly yet earnestly from the heart. Everyone was amazed at the wisdom, power, and depth of his words and at his vast knowledge of Scripture, acquired during the years he spent as an Augustinian friar.

The event catapulted Anthony into a new career as a brilliant preacher and evangelist—a career that he would pursue tirelessly for the rest of his life.

It also brought about his transfer to Bologna, a prominent university city about forty miles away.

Anthony Comes to Bologna

The Franciscan province of Romagna, to which Anthony was now attached, had its headquarters in Bologna. This was where Anthony found a convenient base for his new preaching ministry. Because Anthony's previously hidden gifts were now out in the open, he was soon tapped by the province to teach theology in Bologna to the friars who were preparing for the priesthood.

It was while Anthony was living in Bologna that he received a message from St. Francis, written around 1223. This historic letter granted Anthony permission to teach theology to the friars. The text was short and to the point: "Brother Francis sends his wishes of health to Brother Anthony.... It pleases me that you teach sacred theology to the brothers, as long as—in the words of the Rule—you 'do not extinguish the Spirit of prayer and devotion' with study of this kind."

Eventually, teaching theology to the friars in Bologna ended for Anthony when he was sent as a popular preacher to southern France. A number of heretical groups were afoot in Europe at this time, confusing many with their strange doctrines. Because of Anthony's profound knowledge of Scripture, his training in theology, and his persuasiveness in preaching, he was well equipped to counter these heretical teachings.

Between 1227 and 1230, Anthony served as the provincial minister of Romagna.

ANTHONY SETTLES IN PADUA

During the last two or three years of his short life, Anthony's efforts and zeal as a public preacher were confined, for the most part, to the city of Padua. The crowds that came to see him were often immense, at times reaching an estimated thirty thousand. When churches could not hold such throngs, Anthony had to move outside to the piazzas or open fields. This was especially true when he preached his famous lenten sermons in Padua.

After celebrating Mass and preaching in the mornings, he would hear confessions for long stretches of time. Anthony was tremendously popular with the Paduans, but the work was often exhausting.

TREE HOUSE IN CAMPOSAMPIERO

Finally, Anthony knew he needed a break and more time dedicated to God alone. Perhaps he also sensed that his short life was nearing its end. He was about thirty-six years old at the time.

He withdrew from the city of Padua to the town of Camposampiero, some thirty miles north of Padua. There a nobleman, Count Tiso, had earlier built a hermitage for friars seeking more time for contemplative prayer. With Tiso's help, Anthony had a solitary hut—something like a small tree house—built in the branches of a large walnut tree in a thick forest, not far from the Franciscan hermitage.

The saint spent much of the last weeks and months of his life in that small tree house, praying and working on sermon notes to assist other preachers of the Word.

DYING AT ARCELLA

One day, however, when Anthony came down from the tree to join the other friars for lunch, he began to feel deathly ill. He asked his confreres to take him back to Padua. After laying the saint in an oxcart, the group of friars headed toward Padua.

When they arrived just outside the city, however, they saw that Anthony's condition was worsening. They decided to stop at the Franciscan friary at Arcella, next to a Poor Clare monastery. It was here that St. Anthony would take his last breath.

As his final moments drew near, Anthony received the sacrament of reconciliation and sang a hymn to the Virgin Mary. Then, as noted in the *First Life* (the earliest biography of Anthony), the dying friar looked toward heaven and told a fellow friar, "I see my Lord."

The saint's journey had finally and gloriously ended.

CHAPTER FOUR

St. Anthony, Spiritual Brother of St. Francis
by Carol Ann Morrow

Similarities abound in the lives and legends of St. Francis, the founder of the Franciscans, and St. Anthony, his famous follower. One day, as I heard a friar recount the story of Francis, which I thought I knew well, I heard afresh. What I heard called me to acknowledge how faithfully Anthony listened to the guidance of Francis.

While the logic, even the transparency, of such an observation may be obvious to you, it inspired me all the same. I wanted to draw out the similarities to see where they led me and what they might teach me. I invite you on that journey.

NO TWINS, THESE TWO

The man we call St. Francis of Assisi was also known as the *Poverello*, or "little poor man." Anthony's first biographer, an anonymous Franciscan friar, writes of Anthony that he "was afflicted by a certain natural bulkiness."

When we look back, the authentic words of Francis are none too many, although more than those left behind by many other saints. In addition to the famed "Canticle of the Creatures," we have fewer than a dozen formal letters, a small collection of rules and directives for friars and other followers, plus other prayers. Most of these writings are derived from Scripture.

The humble Francis always called himself unlettered, and his writings were dictated to—and likely edited by—other friars. As Franciscan Fr. Placid Hermann writes in his introduction to the *Writings*, Francis was "not a philosopher given to abstract reasoning. He was a poet and an apostle." Education appears to have made Francis nervous. Anthony might have experienced inner conflicts about education himself, but then he had a lot more learning to be nervous about! While he never lied about his extensive studies he undertook as an Augustinian in Portugal, it was at least a year before any of the friars in Italy knew they had a scholar, preacher, and teacher who had "seemed more skillful in washing kitchen utensils than in expounding the mysteries of Scripture," as that early friar-biographer later muses.

Once the cat was out of the bag, Anthony was asked to teach Scripture to the young friars. Francis knew that his friars would need to preach correctly and well, if only to counter the teachers and preachers who were spreading the Bad News that creation was evil, sex was worse, and sacraments were of dubious value. Anthony became the champion of the Good News—to the friars, to the fallen away, to the faithful. Francis was the poet, Anthony the prose master. I could contrast Deacon Francis with Fr. Anthony, priest and confessor. I could contrast the body of the founder, almost wasted before he breathed his last, with that of Anthony, whose bones showed signs of penance and austerity but whose vocal cords remain incorrupt to this day. We see Francis with the birds and Anthony with the lily. We see Francis with the cross but Anthony with the infant. Between the two, it seems, we've seen it all.

CELEBRATING CIRCUMSTANCES

Francis and Anthony have a lot more in common than *of* as a middle name, to be sure. Both had well-to-do parents—of which each had to let go in more dramatic fashion than has been asked of most of us.

Francis shed his father, along with his clothes, before the bishop of Assisi when he was only a teenager. Anthony may have said more tender good-byes, but he never saw his parents again after he sailed for Morocco in his late twenties. For both men, "Our Father, who art in heaven" was a gospel prayer that rang true to their experience and in their hearts. Knights, crusades, and well-connected parents formed the early sensibilities and imaginations of each man. Francis' father, Pietro, was a merchant who appreciated beauty and value and traveled abroad to import both from France. Anthony's father, according to the "Blue Book" of Portugal, was descended from the Frenchman Godfrey of Bouillon, leader of the First Crusade. (Others doubt this lineage.) Some sources say Anthony's parents served in the royal residence, the Castelo de São Jorge. They certainly lived in its shadow. To me, both saints, despite their talk about being unworthy lowlifes, reveal a sense of great personal dignity. They bowed before God, but they walked tall. Both were popular as youths.

The Middle Ages found both men in the midst of territorial battles. Francis went to fight in the battles to preserve the city autonomy, a political movement gaining strength in medieval Italy—and ended up a prisoner of war. Anthony saw much evidence of border disputes and transfers of power as the Muslim influence waxed and waned in Portugal. Later, both were intent on preaching the gospel to the Muslims, or Saracens. The two idealists became spiritual knights under a banner of freedom for the soul.

The Fourth Lateran Council (1215) was a pivotal event in Church history for these two medieval saints. In its first session, the Council Fathers treated two major issues: the Holy Land and the era's "protestants," known as the Cathars ("pure") or Albigensians (after Albi, France, a major stronghold). These themes shape every follower of Francis, who so loved the land where Jesus was born and wanted everyone to know and live the gospel.

GREAT LOVES OF GREAT SAINTS

As is true of many other saints, both Francis and Anthony took a while to discern their basic path in life. (This may console many college students in search of a major.) Francis thought he was supposed to repair church buildings. Instead he was to restore the Catholic Church, which was in disrepair from bad example and misguided teachers. Anthony thought he was to be an Augustinian, but that was only a first step toward becoming a Franciscan. Both stumbled, doubted, and rebounded. Both men wanted to be martyrs; both were denied a martyr's death. Both experienced stormy seas as they attempted to evangelize the Muslims. Francis was insulted, beaten, and threatened by the sultan of Egypt, but he was not killed. In fact, he eventually gained the Egyptian leader's respect.

The heroic martyrdom of the Franciscans in Morocco drew Anthony to become a friar. While he followed their trail, inheriting their mission to Morocco, he fell ill with a fever either on the sea journey or soon after his arrival. Sick for months, he nearly died, but not at the hands of Muslims. Eventually, he arrived in Sicily and made his way north.

Both men loved the hermit life; neither had much chance to savor it. Thomas Celano, early biographer of Francis, writes: "Francis was often suspended in such sweetness of contemplation that, caught up out of himself, he could not reveal what he had experienced because it went beyond all human comprehension." He was often taxed, however, by the demands of leading his fledgling religious order—and observing canonical requirements such as writing a rule.

Anthony spent about one year as a hermit at Monte Paolo near Forli, Italy, before his public gifts were discovered. Near his death, he tried again for the quiet life but, despite his having taken refuge in the walnut tree, people sought him out for counsel and confession.

Though each saint treasured solitude, each balanced the inward life with love and solicitude for other people, even involving themselves in civic concerns. In Francis' "Canticle of the Creatures," verses 10 and 11 (about pardon and peace) were added some time after the earlier verses to effect and celebrate reconciliation between the bishop of Assisi and the *podesta*, or mayor. Francis actually directed this peacemaking project from his bed of illness.

Anthony, too, "called back to brotherly peace those who disagreed with each other and gave freedom to those who were imprisoned. He required that whatever was taken in usury or through violence be restituted," writes his earliest biographer. Other chroniclers describe Anthony's personal efforts to free a Paduan politician, who was being held prisoner by the head of the opposition. Anthony walked from Padua to Verona to beg mercy for the prisoner. He was not able to count this among his successes, however.

The two saints also shared a warm affection for Sister Earth. While Francis is the official patron of the environment, Anthony evidenced a strong affection for the earth as well.

While Francis preached to the birds, Anthony held the attention of the fish. Air and sea were covered by this pair; they also connected with the creatures on dry land! St. Bonaventure (in the *Major Life*) describes Francis' pet sheep, which knelt during the friars' prayers and bowed profoundly during the Consecration of the Mass.

St. Anthony's biographers include the story of a donkey that, hungry though it was, knelt before the Eucharist rather than head straight for the hay it was offered. Both stories give a vivid sense of faith in the Eucharist, in contrast to the Cathars' mistrust of sacramentality.

Both saints had a strong sense of place. Francis felt especially drawn to Mount La Verna; Anthony sought refuge in a tree at Camposampiero. Yet, when Sister Death was approaching, both men longed to be "home."

St. Bonaventure writes that Francis "asked to be brought to St. Mary of the Portiuncula, so that he might yield up his spirit where he had first received the spirit of grace." Francis even asked to be stripped of his clothes so that he could lie directly on the earth!

Anthony, when he knew that he was dying, asked the friars to carry him back to his beloved Padua. He actually died nearby at Arcella, since the journey by cart proved too painful and difficult. Traditional paintings show him blessing Padua's horizon from his traveling bed of pain, just as Francis blessed Assisi before his death.

Perfect Joy Among the Brothers

While I could link still more stories of two men born in different nations with different gifts and temperaments, you've got the idea by now, I suspect.

So what to make of it all? Is Anthony simply a copycat saint? Is Francis so powerful a leader that his imprint is visible in everyone inspired by him?

I think it's far more profound and beautiful than that. I sense that the work of becoming holy, my task and yours, shapes distinct individuals. Just as Pentecost celebrates the Spirit's expression in many languages (see Acts 2:5–11), we express grace in myriad ways today. We are formed by environment and grace, by politics and prayer, by church and conscience. All God's creatures conspire to teach us as well. We stumble. We stutter. We rise. We are lifted.

To read the written words of each of these saints is to reread the Bible, particularly the Gospels. To follow each man's footsteps—and the message of each man's actions—is to be on the path of Christ. Francis and Anthony are alike because they were shaped by the words and actions of Jesus.

This isn't some biographical nicety. This is what I should have expected! This is what I should expect of myself! Francis and Anthony are brothers to one another because they are such close kin to their Creator.

In a charming—if apocryphal—story found in *The Little Flowers of St. Francis*, the saint is teaching his beloved Br. Leo how to find perfect joy. It's not in giving good example, not in being a healer or miracle worker, not in knowledge and prophecy, insists Francis. As he walks, he keeps describing wonderful spiritual gifts, all the while denying that they are the source of perfect joy. Finally, an exasperated Br. Leo asks Francis, "Father, I beg you to tell me where perfect joy is."

Br. Leo receives a long, long answer in which Francis describes exposure to rain, cold, mud, and hunger, and then knocking at the door of their headquarters only to hear, "Who are you?"

The porter doesn't recognize Francis and his companions then and leaves them out in the cold—not once, but three times—each time with more force and even violence. "If we endure all those evils and insults and blows with joy and patience, reflecting that we must accept and bear the sufferings of the Blessed Christ patiently for love of him," Francis concludes, "Oh, Brother Leo, write: 'That is perfect joy!'"

In the light of that Franciscan parable, we can see that Francis surely takes a lot of pleasure in granting Anthony the prominence he has in many circles. And Anthony surely feels humbled in return!

For both saints, perfect joy is defined not by the number of their devotees, or by how many churches or magazines are named for them, but by seeing that Jesus becomes visible in every age. I'm reminded of Paul writing to the Corinthians about the role of God's ministers: "I planted, Apollos watered, but God gave the growth" (1 Corinthians 3:6). Just so, Francis planted, Anthony watered, but God gives the increase.

PART TWO

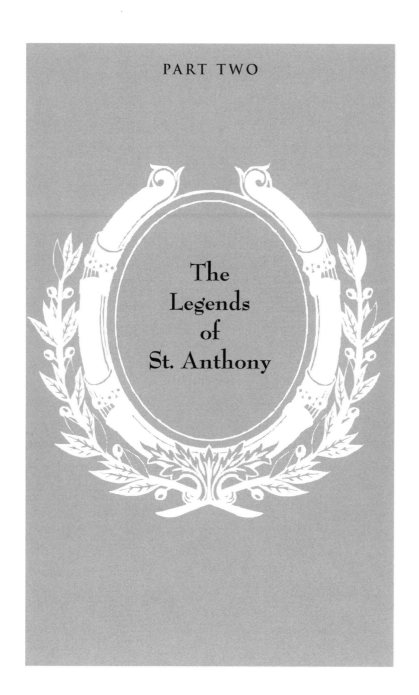

The
Legends
of
St. Anthony

CHAPTER FIVE

How to View the Legends of St. Anthony

by Leonard Foley, O.F.M.

D evotion to Anthony began while he was still living and spread quickly after his death. Legends and stories of his life multiplied, as they often do with popular saints. The question arises: Which legends are true?

In our day, historians examine the past using a strictly scientific method. World-famous and most conscientious theologian Fr. Ignatius Brady, O.F.M., has written, "I may seem a bit 'modern' but there is no need to dwell on legends when there are so many proven miracles that have been worked by his [Anthony's] intercession…. The Christ-Child is closer to Anthony and all of us if we are living in God's grace than if he were a baby in our arms. So the story is still 'true' even if it is a legend."

LEAVE ROOM FOR A LITTLE POETRY

Legends and stories are the poetry of childlike faith. They arise among people who feel no inhibition about using their imagination. Even as scientific hagiographers watch them over their glasses, they are not afraid to let the line between fact and story blur—it's practically impossible to find that line anyway. The poetry of the simple (a stumbling block to the wise) warms the solemn declarations and abstract phrases of the creeds.

The makers of legend let their minds soar through the skies of wonder. They know the dogmas that are engraved in granite: Jesus is true God and true man; God is One and Trinity; we are saved by the death and Resurrection of Jesus that is re-presented at every Eucharist. But they are not loath to embellish with little cherubs the majestic picture of Jesus rising from the dead. If God wants you to find your false teeth through the prayer of St. Anthony, I say wonderful. *Deo gratias!*

By way of understanding the story-weaving of Catholic tradition, do you remember the sisters teaching the story of the boy Jesus making sparrows out of mud? How he clapped his hands and they flew away? We've all heard that St. Christopher bore the infant Jesus over a raging stream: The name meant "Christ-bearer." We "know" there was a little door at the back of heaven where Mary let sinners in, after St. Peter barred them from the pearly gates. We recall that St. Scholastica prayed for rain and that the resulting flood from heaven made it impossible for her brother St. Benedict to leave her convent—which was her wish all the while. And so forth.

God forbid that this would become the basis of faith and we would ever abandon systematic and logical theology. It, after all, also uses the wide-ranging power of imagination. But it seems evident that human nature needs some over-the-back-fence theology that is not quite so stern and unrelieved—coffee-klatch poetry that suggests but does not prove. Legends are comforting where dogma is reassuring. And sometimes legends, in addition to being good teaching aids, are just plain fun—something that should never be in short supply among the children of God.

Jesus *could have* made mud sparrows fly. Whether he actually met Peter sneaking out of Rome doesn't matter: His prescience was a challenge to Peter's conscience. Mary isn't in charge of a black-market back door to heaven, but she is a motherly symbol of the mercy of God. And *every* person who lifts another person's spirits and "carries" them through troubled times is named "Christopher" in those imaginary record books in heaven.

WHY ST. ANTHONY'S POPULARITY?

It's easy to see why some saints attract people with certain needs: Mary for both mothers and celibates, Joseph for workers, Mother Teresa for those who care for the most abandoned of the poor. But what can explain the almost universal cult of St. Anthony? We don't know a whole lot of details about his life beyond the bare-bones outline given in the first chapter. We do have his sermons. But, apart from the legends, his life was what every Christian's life is meant to be, only writ large—a steady courage to face the ups and downs of life and the call to love and forgive, to be concerned for the needs of others, to deal with crises great and small, and to have our feet solidly on the ground of total, trusting love and dependence on God.

Why his popularity, then? At least some of the stories must be literally true. He must have had an overpowering effect on the people of his day. He must have been an authentic saint.

The legends abound. Bring the fishes' heads above water. Have them dance, if you want to. Let the donkeys kneel down before Jesus, even sing the Our Father.

But aren't there dangers here? Certainly. I have seen people enter a church, completely ignore the reserved sacrament, and go directly to kneel before Anthony's statue. I have seen, in an Asian country, people jamming the streets around a church on a weekday night when a certain novena was to be held. The following Sunday, the street was almost empty. I suppose there are people who, to put it bluntly, seem to have more faith in Anthony than in Jesus.

These practices certainly don't suit the saint they are intended to honor! The greatest danger is attributing to a saint what *only God can do*. No one can save your soul but God in Jesus and the Spirit. God's grace—that is, the total, unconditional love surrounding every human being—comes only from God. We ask the saints in heaven to pray for us, just as we ask some earthly saints (and even some who may not qualify) to pray for us. But none of them "grants grace."

SAINTS MAKE GOD'S LOVE VISIBLE

All right, some will say, in a familiar line of argument, why not go straight to God? Jesus is the universal and only savior. By all means, let us go to God first, make Jesus the center. But we are human, and God is invisible, and so is Jesus—for now. So God sends us brothers and sisters who are—or at least are called to be—warm, supportive, comforting. They make God's love visible—the ones still with us and those who have gone ahead. They are sacraments—small *s*—of God's love.

Perhaps we may say that in the great river that is our faith and religion and the solid truths of revelation, there are some shallows next to the shore. These are the meandering legends and stories that feed the main stream. When it gets too deep for us, we can play along the side for a while. That's human and understandable, as long as we know the river's source.

There are overwhelming facts in Jesus' life, especially his miracles, his fearless denunciation of hypocrisy, his death and Resurrection. But he also made gallons of wine for a wedding celebration. And anyone who thinks he never played a trick or two on Joseph and Mary should take a course under Dr. Bill Cosby. I think St. Anthony would say about all the legends and stories: "Let's have balance, but imagination too, just as we have Shakespeare and 'Casey at the Bat'; Beethoven, but also a little schmaltz."

But St. Anthony of Padua would also say, "Fight error with courage and kindness. Look around you and see the injustice that chains so many people. Take time for quiet prayer. Know your faith and let that knowledge burst into flame in your heart."

CHAPTER SIX

Why St. Anthony Holds the Child Jesus

by Jack Wintz, O.F.M.

Next to Mary of Nazareth, the saint most often seen in artwork holding the child Jesus in his arms is St. Anthony of Padua. If there is anything I've learned from visiting churches and Catholic missions throughout the world, it is that the image of Anthony and the child Jesus is a favorite around the globe. It can be found wherever Catholic missionaries have carried the Good News, even in the most remote regions of the world.

Since I grew up in a Franciscan parish (in southern Indiana) and was then educated in the Franciscan seminary system, I was very familiar with that image. How could I avoid it? And yet for most of my life, I seldom asked others or myself: "*Why* is St. Anthony presented that way?"

I have consistently found the image of Anthony with the child Jesus quite friendly and likable. Even as I encountered artists who smiled at it in patronizing ways and dismissed it as too sweet and sentimental, this did not keep me from finding the image appealing.

For a good part of my life, I did not look for a deeper meaning in this familiar image. Nor did I ask why the image caught the popular fancy of almost every culture around the world.

Looking for the Deeper Meanings

In recent years, however, I've taken a wholly different viewpoint. I've concluded that this popular image has developed in the

Franciscan tradition and in the Catholic consciousness for some profound reason. For me, it conveys something vitally important in the Franciscan and Catholic spirit.

Exploring this image is something like exploring a vivid dream we've had during the night. We wake up the next morning and wonder, "Now what was that all about?" We assume that this dream, emerging from our inner depths, may hold an important meaning for our lives. So, too, the images that rise from the inner life of the Church may well hold profound meanings for us.

It is interesting to note that, although Anthony has been frequently portrayed in art since his death in 1231, images of him *with the Christ child* did not become popular until the seventeenth century.

Before exploring the depiction of Anthony and the Christ child, however, we should look at one of the popular stories explaining the origin of the custom. A good number of Franciscan historians, I believe, would advise us to approach the story as legend rather than as solid historical fact.

According to one version of the legend—and there are many— there was a Count Tiso who had a castle about eleven miles from Padua. And on the grounds of the castle the count had provided a chapel and a hermitage for the friars.

Anthony often went there toward the end of his life and spent time praying in one of the hermit cells. One night, his little cell suddenly filled up with light. Jesus, in the form of a tiny child, appeared to Anthony. Passing by the hermitage, the count saw the light shining from the room and St. Anthony holding and communicating with the infant.

The count fell to his knees on seeing this wondrous sight. And when the vision ended, Anthony saw the count kneeling at the open door. Anthony begged Count Tiso not to reveal what he had seen until after his death.

Whether this story be legend or fact, the image of Anthony with the child Jesus has important truths to teach us.

Anthony's Franciscan Ties

First of all, we notice that Anthony is wearing a Franciscan habit. Seeing him as a true son of St. Francis and a part of the Franciscan tradition is very important.

It is a historical fact that Anthony joined the Order of Friars Minor while Francis was still alive. We know that Anthony attended the Franciscan chapter of Pentecost 1221 at which Francis was also present. Although more than two thousand friars came to that famous gathering near Assisi, it's hard to believe that Anthony—famous for finding lost objects for everyone else!—would not have been resourceful enough to find a way to see and hear the much loved and illustrious founder of the Franciscan brotherhood, or perhaps even meet him. Less than three years later, Anthony received a personal letter from Francis graciously granting him permission to teach theology to the friars.

What I'm getting at is that Anthony, being a committed member of Francis' order, would have known well the spirit, teachings, values, and dramatic actions of Francis. Like the other friars, he would have surely heard about Francis' famous celebration of Christmas near Greccio, Italy, in 1223.

On that occasion, St. Francis had people come to Midnight Mass in a cave where there was an ox and an ass and a manger filled with straw. And the story went around that the Christ child appeared in the straw and that Francis held the child in his arms. How interesting! The story of the baby Jesus appearing to Anthony is a kind of "copycat" story, amazingly similar to that of St. Francis.

Even more important is the attitude or theology behind the story. Francis, we know, was tremendously impressed by the "poverty" and littleness of God—a God who left behind his divinity and chose to become a vulnerable child. Francis saw, in God's entering the human race as a little baby on Christmas Day, a God of unbelievable generosity, a God who held nothing back from human beings, a God of total self-giving, humility, and poverty.

The *poverty of God* made a strong impression on St. Francis, according to evidence in his Rule. In the sixth chapter he instructs his followers that they should "serve the Lord in Poverty…because the Lord *made himself poor* for us in this world."

Anthony would have read this rule often. More than that, he would have taken to heart the larger spiritual vision of St. Francis, which extended beyond his fascination with the feast of Christmas. St. Francis also saw God's poverty and vulnerability and self-giving love in Jesus' suffering and death, so much so that he often broke into tears at the sight of a cross. He saw God's poverty in the Eucharist as well, where under the common forms of bread and wine Jesus humbly hands his whole self over to those he loves.

To see St. Anthony holding the infant Jesus in his arms, therefore, is to see a true follower of St. Francis. For did not Francis also embrace that same image of God's vulnerability and humble love?

An Eloquent Preacher Holding Up the Word

Another meaningful way to interpret the presence of the Christ child in the arms of St. Anthony is to realize that Anthony was a great preacher of the gospel—a brilliant communicator of the Incarnate Word. In his sermons, Anthony emphasized the mystery of the Incarnation.

In 1946, Pope Pius XII officially declared Anthony a doctor of the Universal Church, with the designation "Doctor of the Gospel." Clearly, Anthony had taught Scripture with great power and effectiveness.

This leads us to view in a whole new light the images of Anthony holding the infant: Through his Scripture-based preaching, the real, historical Anthony was holding and communicating to the world the Incarnate Word of God. Very often the infant in Anthony's arms is portrayed as standing on the holy Bible. Can there be a more obvious symbol and clue that the Christ child in Anthony's arms represents the very embodiment of the Word of God? Often, the child stands on the Bible's open pages as if rising out of the printed word itself.

In San Antonio, Texas, there is a large and lovely statue of St. Anthony of Padua, the patron saint of the city. It was a gift from Portugal (Anthony's birthplace) to San Antonio. It stands along the famous San Antonio Riverwalk bordering the San Antonio River in the heart of the city. The Christ child in Anthony's arms stands on the Bible, and his arms are extended in the shape of the cross as if embracing the whole world—as if Anthony is saying, "I hold up to all, as Savior of the world, this humble God of self-emptying love!"

St. Anthony's Abbreviated Message

In the Christian literature and piety of the Middle Ages, one finds the idea of the abbreviated word of God (*verbum abbreviatum*, in Latin). Among the many medieval religious figures influenced by this idea was St. Francis of Assisi. In chapter nine of his Rule (his instructions for his followers written in 1223), Francis exhorted his "brothers that when they preach, their words be well considered… and brief, because our Lord, when on earth, kept his words brief [*quia verbum abbreviatum fecit Dominus super terram*]." A literal translation of the Latin would be "because the Lord made an abbreviated (or shortened) word on earth."

For Christians, the word *word* can have various meanings. For example, when Francis speaks of the Lord keeping his words brief, he is probably referring to Jesus' preaching—and to Jesus' using few words to communicate profound ideas. Jesus' preaching is often short and to the point. He sums up his whole message in short sentences such as "Love one another as I have loved you," (John 15:12) or "Love the Lord your God with all your heart… and…your neighbor as yourself" (Matthew 22:37). Indeed, in the last example, his brief instruction summarizes "all the law and the prophets" (Matthew 22:40).*

Regarding God the Father, we can refer to God as 1) speaking many words, as in the Old Testament or 2) speaking the one Word made flesh in the New Testament. In the latter example we are referring to the Divine Word who entered history as the Incarnate Word, Jesus Christ, who was conceived by the Holy Spirit in the womb of the Virgin Mary and born in Bethlehem of Judea. The Letter to the Hebrews in its opening verses compares the idea of the many words and the one Word: "Long ago God spoke to our ancestors in many and various ways by the prophets, but in these last days he has spoken to us by a Son, whom he appointed heir of all things, through whom he also created the worlds" (Hebrews 1:1–2). As hinted here, this Divine Word also existed before the world was made as the eternal Word of God, and Son of God.

By way of summary: The Son of God, out of love for humanity, came to this earth in the form of a vulnerable human child. In this process of self-emptying love, the divine Word shortened (or abbreviated) himself, so to speak, to the size of a baby lying in a manger. Such was the humility of God as revealed at the Incarnation. We gaze in wonder on the tiny infant, the Word made flesh, in the crude manger. Lying there in great humility is the *Verbum abbreviatum*, the abbreviated Word.

In the sermons of St. Anthony, especially those touching on the mystery of the Incarnation, Anthony himself uses this kind

I must give great credit to my confrere Fr. Michael Guinan, O.F.M., professor of sacred Scripture and of biblical spirituality at the Franciscan School of Theology in Berkeley, California, for giving me much help and guidance in developing this section on St. Anthony and the "abbreviated Word of God."

of "God-reduced-to-smallness" image. In sermon 3, section 7, for example, Anthony expressed amazement at "the Lord of the Universe: wrapped in swaddling clothes" and at "the King of Angels: lying in the stable." And in sermon 3, section 10, we have the awesome thought that "the one whose name is boundless is laid in a narrow manger."

And so we return to the image of the infant in St. Anthony's arms. This infant, like the infant of the "narrow manger," says it all. If you are looking for the whole meaning of the Incarnation in a nutshell, here you have it. Indeed, if you are looking for an abbreviated sermon or "short word" on the whole meaning of the love of God and the love of Christ, look at the infant in the arms of St. Anthony. The divine infant represents—in abbreviated form—the totality of the Good News.

All around the world—wherever the image of Anthony with the infant is seen—we can admire this great Franciscan preacher. He is truly living the Rule of St. Francis and proclaiming the gospel through the Incarnate Word himself, simply by holding up the Christ child, who has made himself small for love of us.

WE, TOO, CAN CARRY CHRIST

The image of Anthony holding the Divine Infant is a symbol and model for each of us. The image inspires us to go through life clinging to the wonderful mystery of the humble, self-emptying Christ, who accompanies us as a servant of our humanity and of the world's healing.

This is the image of Christ that St. Paul sketches for us in his Letter to the Philippians. Paul urges that we take on the attitude of "Christ Jesus, who, though he was in the form of God, did not regard equality with God as something to be exploited, but emptied himself, taking the form of a slave, being born in human likeness.

And being found in human form, he humbled himself and became obedient to the point of death—even death on a cross" (2:5–8).

This passage from Philippians is a key building block of Franciscan spirituality. And if the infant in Anthony's arms were to speak, Philippians 2:5–8 would be his first message and self-description.

Just as Jesus' death on a cross reveals God's total self-giving love for us, so also does his Incarnation (symbolized in the Christ child). The late Fr. Raymond Brown, eminent Scripture scholar, has affirmed that "the divine self-giving" revealed in Jesus' Incarnation is comparable to "God's supreme act of love...embodied in Jesus' self-giving on the cross." Brown adds, "Indeed, some theologians have so appreciated the intensity of love in the Incarnation that they have wondered whether that alone might not have saved the world even if Jesus was never crucified."

This is the kind of love that radiates from the Christ child so often pictured in St. Anthony's arms. Would it not be a good idea for all of us to go through life carrying an imaginary God-child in our arms—and holding him up to the world?

The child, however, is not really imaginary or fictitious. Two thousand years ago, thanks to the Virgin Mary's "Yes," the Son of God left behind his divine condition and came to dwell as a human child among us. Our faith tells us that he *does* accompany us each day like a humble servant—like a vulnerable child.

Like St. Anthony, we do well lovingly to carry this image with us on our journey through life.

PART THREE

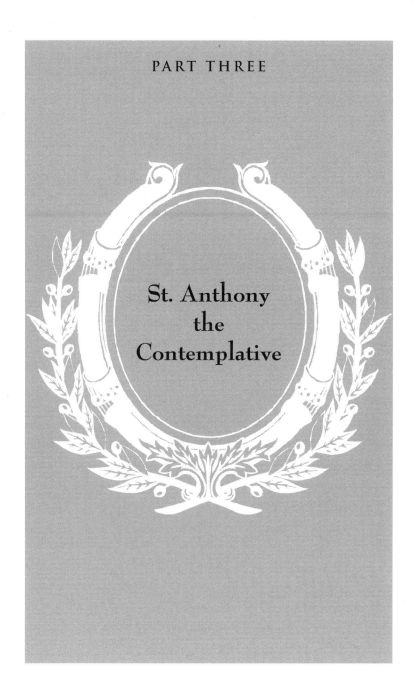

St. Anthony
the
Contemplative

CHAPTER SEVEN

St. Anthony, the Contemplative

by Jack Wintz, O.F.M.

It was not until the year 2002 that I discovered the very first book ever written about St. Anthony of Padua. It's an extraordinary little work that was published in Latin in 1232, but apparently it had no English translation until 1984. The title used for this first life of St. Anthony was simply the *First Life* (*Vita Prima* in Latin) or the *Assidua* (because *assidua* happens to be the first word of the little book). *First Life* was published one year after Anthony's death, which occurred on June 13, 1231.

A Franciscan friar, who chose to remain anonymous, wrote this short biography at the request of his community for the occasion of St. Anthony's canonization (in 1232). Since it was written so soon after his death and by a confrere who obviously knew the saint, the book is considered a reliable source for the basic facts of Anthony's life.

One thing that jumped out at me in my first reading of this book was that Anthony was truly a contemplative. I don't mean this in the sense that he totally left the world and became a lifelong hermit or a cloistered monk who never stepped outside the walls of his monastery. Rather, he was a contemplative in the sense that he possessed a desire or longing to search for the face of God and to live totally for God—and he pursued that inner longing with noticeable frequency throughout his life. As we shall see, the longing never really left him.

Previously, we noted that this had also been true of St. Francis of Assisi, whose example Anthony was certainly following. Both Francis and Anthony had this contemplative thirst, this need to seek God often in solitude so as to live for God alone. In the pages of the *First Life*, as well as in other sources, we certainly see this need in Anthony. Time and again, Anthony simply experienced the need to step aside from his regular activities and to search for God in solitary places such as caves or little hermitages. And he did this for rather long stretches of time. This chapter is something of a retracing of Anthony's life but with a heavy emphasis on the saint's contemplative search.

ANTHONY'S CONTEMPLATIVE SEARCH BEGINS EARLY

Anyone who looks carefully through the pages of the *First Life* will notice both strong as well as subtle signs of Anthony's contemplative temperament. We learn very quickly that his parents lived in Lisbon and close to the cathedral church. They "gave him the name Fernando at the holy font of baptism," says the *First Life*. "Indeed, they entrusted him to this church," the book adds in its early pages, "so that he learn the sacred writings there." Here already we have a strong clue of early opportunities provided the saint by his faith-filled parents to search devoutly for God in the pages of the Bible under the guidance of the cathedral clergy.

Then, at age fifteen, according to the *First Life*, Ferdinand withdrew from the world and entered the Augustinian monastery nearby—another clear sign of his early longing to seek the face of God before all else. After living in this monastery for two years, he sought to find an even better climate for his contemplative search. Ferdinand still found that his search for God in Lisbon was compromised because his old friends kept trying to visit him at the monastery. As a result, and as if to reinforce his desire for a "more fruitful tranquility," Ferdinand asked his superiors to transfer him to the Augustinian monastery in the city of Coimbra, the capital of Portugal at the time, one hundred miles north of Lisbon.

In Coimbra, he cultivated his inner life with frequent meditation and the reading of Scripture, "examining…the deep sense of God's words" as well as "the words of the saints with diligent inquiry. And, indeed," the *First Life* adds, "he entrusted to his tenacious memory whatever he read so that in short time he was able to acquire a knowledge of the Scriptures that no one else hoped to possess."

THE SAINT'S JOURNEY TAKES A SURPRISING TURN

As previously explained, Ferdinand's journey toward God, however, soon jumped to a new level of intensity. It happened that the relics of five holy Franciscan martyrs, beheaded in Morocco for preaching Christianity to the Muslims, were brought to Coimbra amid great publicity and fervor. On learning about the great faith and heroism of these Franciscan martyrs, Ferdinand felt strongly inspired to follow in their footsteps.

Not far from the monastery where Ferdinand was staying, there happened to live a group of Franciscan friars at the church of St. Anthony. They often came begging at the door of the Augustinian monastery where Ferdinand was staying. He spoke earnestly to the Franciscans about his desire to become a Franciscan, especially if they would promise to send him to Morocco to become a martyr for Christ. With great joy, the friars said that, in two days, they could invest him in the Franciscan habit.

As mentioned earlier, Ferdinand, the Augustinian, became Anthony, the Franciscan. He took the name in honor of St. Anthony of Egypt, the patron of the church where he was living with the other Franciscans. Choosing this name is yet another clue that the contemplative life had a special appeal for him. St. Anthony of Egypt was a famous fourth-century hermit, considered to be one of the early founders of monasticism. Anthony of Egypt had spent long years in the desert and other isolated places, giving himself over to contemplative prayer.

But contemplation did not seem to be the main priority of the young Franciscan friar at that moment. He was eager to embark for Morocco to evangelize the Muslims, even at the risk of losing his own life out of love for Christ.

ANTHONY'S DREAM IS FRUSTRATED

Anthony, however, became deathly sick in Morocco and had to sail back to Portugal to regain his health. On the journey home, a strong wind swept the ship badly off course and it landed in Sicily.

We can only imagine how his failure to carry out his mission of preaching to the Muslims was a devastating blow for him. He must have felt a great sense of humiliation and embarrassment in falling so short of his grand dreams, even if it was because of serious illness. And exactly what kind of illness was it? Was it a physical illness such as malaria? Or could it have been the result of what to some modern eyes might seem a kind of psychological phenomenon, such as culture shock or a sudden loss of confidence? We may never know for sure.

Up to this time, however, Anthony seemed to be on the fast track toward spiritual perfection. He was a bright light as an Augustinian friar and a student of the Scriptures and of other theological courses. He showed great initiative in asking to be sent to Coimbra, where the discipline was harder and where his talents and religious zeal could shine. Then he opted for a greater challenge still: Joining this new Franciscan brotherhood—spreading like wildfire across Europe—and personally setting off with great confidence to imitate those heroic martyrs whose bones had been carried triumphantly into Coimbra. Maybe this humbling experience led Anthony to the insight that he had to rely less on his own human wisdom and talents and more on the saving power of God. Maybe he had to learn the spiritual wisdom hidden in the psalmist's words: "Unless the Lord builds the house, those who build it labor in vain" (Psalm 127:1).

ANTHONY RECOVERS HIS HEALTH AND CONTEMPLATIVE PATH

In any case, we can assume that Anthony was still sick or down in the dumps when he reached the coast of Sicily. The friars there did what they could to nurse him back to wholeness. They encouraged him to go along with them to the chapter of Pentecost 1221 near Assisi. The order's founder, St. Francis of Assisi himself, was there.

Because Anthony was a newcomer to the order, the chapter event ended without his receiving any assignment. We can imagine that during the chapter Anthony may have been keeping a very low profile, being perhaps not too eager to talk about his failed, first missionary adventure. It is to his credit that he persevered as a friar during this challenging time. One thing we learn from the *First Life* is that, before the meeting ended, Anthony had the courage to introduce himself to the head friar of the Romagna province in northern Italy and to ask to travel back to Romagna with him to learn more about the Franciscan way of life.

The *First Life* describes Anthony's humble attitude in these words: "He neither mentioned his studies nor boasted of the churchly ministry he had exercised; instead, out of love for Christ, hiding all his knowledge and intelligence, he declared that he wished to know, thirst for, and embrace only Christ, and him crucified." Seeing Anthony's single-minded devotion to Christ, the provincial agreed to take him to Romagna. The saint soon rediscovered his contemplative soul. As the *First Life* tells us: "When Anthony, through God's disposition, reached the place [Romagna], he devoutly retired…to the hermitage of Monte Paolo, where he entered into the peace of silence.

More than ever, Anthony went searching for the contemplative space he needed to reinforce his union with God and to regain peace of heart—and to sort out all the things going on inside himself since the day he sailed off so confidently to Morocco. Just as he was pondering these things, he learned about a secluded cell that a certain friar had built nearby. He asked the friar to let him use it. When the friar agreed, Anthony went there daily for a lengthy stretch of time to quiet his soul and to search again for the face of God. He took with him, the *First Life* informs us, only "some bread and a small container of water."

A New Career Is Launched

One day, after significant time had passed, Anthony went with some other friars to an ordination ceremony in Forlì. A good number of Franciscan and Dominican friars were there for the occasion. The local superior asked several Dominicans to address those assembled, but all refused. Finally, the *First Life* informs us, "The superior turned to Friar Anthony and ordered him to proclaim to those assembled whatever the Holy Spirit might suggest to him."

Anthony obeyed and humbly preached to those present. As he spoke, everyone was amazed at the wisdom and power of his message. Now upon hearing him preach, they were astonished by the "unexpected depth of his words" and "the spirit with which he spoke" as well as by his vast knowledge of the Bible.

This event catapulted Anthony into an incredible career as a preacher and evangelist. The *First Life* draws a clear cause-and-effect link between his commitment to contemplation and his power as a preacher. Of Anthony, the book says: "The faithful dweller of the hermitage was sent out into the world and his lips, closed for so long [in silent contemplation], were opened to proclaim the glory of God."

For several years Anthony preached throughout northern Italy and southern France. At one point, the minister general sent him to the papal court in Rome to preach to the pope and other Church leaders. To quote the *First Life* again, "Anthony's words were heard with the warmest devotion by the supreme pontiff." Anthony "drew out of Scripture such original and profound meaning, that he was called by the pope himself...'the Ark of the Testament.'"

THE CONTEMPLATIVE CALL IS NEVER FAR AWAY

Quite often, even during Anthony's busy life as a preacher, as well as during his term as a provincial minister of northern Italy, he would answer the call to take care of his contemplative needs. In his book *St. Anthony: Doctor of the Church* (1973), Sophronius Clasen, O.F.M., mentions at least two places to which Anthony would retire from time to time for solitude and contemplation. One of them was in the woods of Monteluco near Spoleto. According to Clasen, Anthony would climb the mountain south of town and, after walking an hour, would reach "the unassuming old chapel which the Benedictines had given to the friars." The friars had built a mud dwelling close to the chapel, and in the great oak forest nearby they had found a few caves on the side of the mountain. Here they could pray undisturbed. And as they gazed down on the beauties of Umbria, which lay at the foot of the mountain, they praised God as the mighty Creator of this wondrous world. Clasen writes that "Anthony had a grotto assigned to him in this place. Even now we can read the inscription in it which tells us that he dwelt there: 'This is the grotto in which St. Anthony did penance.'"

Anthony had an even more special affection for Mount La Verna as a place for withdrawing from time to time to satisfy his contemplative yearnings. As Clasen points out, Anthony shared St. Francis' love for the hidden caves of this mountaintop retreat in northern Italy, where Francis had received the five wounds of Christ. Anthony loved praying in one of the little caves on the mountain. In memory of Anthony's visits, the cave has been transformed, in more recent times, into the Oratory of St. Anthony. And it is still a popular stop for La Verna visitors today.

In St. Anthony's sermons, Clasen finds further evidence and clues of the saint's great love and appreciation for contemplative prayer. To cite Anthony's own words: "The taste of God in contemplation is more precious than everything else; for, no matter what a man might wish for, it is nothing when compared to this. For, when the spirit of a man stands before God and sees his happiness and tastes his delights, then in truth has he attained to paradise."

A Contemplative to the End

During the last two years of his life, St. Anthony's demanding labors as a popular preacher and confessor were confined mainly to the city of Padua. The crowds who came to see him were at times huge, often reaching thirty thousand. To make room for such multitudes, Anthony had to move outside to the open fields. Seeing the importance of keeping on course spiritually, even given his hectic schedule, he made sure he had opportunities to get away to pray in places of solitude. One of these places, of course, was his little cave at Mount La Verna. These experiences helped revitalize Anthony, allowing him to return to his preaching with a renewed spirit.

Finally, Anthony foresaw that his life was coming to a close despite his young age of thirty-six. He withdrew from the city of Padua in search, once again, for a place more conducive to contemplation. This led him to the nearby town of Camposampiero. With the help of a certain nobleman named Tiso, a solitary hut—something like a small tree house—was built for Anthony in the branches of a walnut tree in a thick forest, not far from a Franciscan friary. The saint spent the last weeks and months of his life in that little hut or cell. "In this cell," as we read in the *First Life*, "the servant of God led a truly solitary life and dedicated himself to exercises of holy contemplation."

One day, however, when Anthony came down from the tree to join the other friars for lunch, he became seriously ill. He asked his confreres to take him by cart to Padua. When they got just outside Padua, however, the group decided to stop at the Franciscan friary at Arcella, next to a Poor Clare monastery. It was here that Anthony would breathe his last.

As the friar's final moments drew near, he received the sacrament of reconciliation for the last time and "sang a hymn to the glorious Virgin." When he finished the hymn, the *First Life* relates, the dying friar "suddenly raised his eyes toward heaven and with a stunned look, stared in front of himself for a long time. When the friar who was supporting him asked what he saw, he answered, 'I see my Lord.'"

Now, at last, Anthony's contemplative longing to see the face of God was successfully and gloriously fulfilled!

CHAPTER EIGHT

Five Favorite Hideaways of St. Anthony
by Jack Wintz, O.F.M.

It is clear to me that St. Anthony, deep down, had a profound need to be a contemplative—a person seeking intimate union with God. In October 2006, while spending several weeks traveling between Assisi and Padua, I had an opportunity to visit five of St. Anthony's favorite hideaways—that is, five of his favorite places for contemplative prayer.

Anthony's career as a brilliant preacher, you may recall, was launched during an ordination ceremony in the Italian town of Forlì. A good number of Franciscans and Dominicans were at the ceremony. The local superior invited several Dominicans to preach. When they begged off, the superior turned to Anthony and insisted that he share with the invited guests whatever the Holy Spirit might prompt him to say. Anthony rose to the occasion and preached so inspiringly that he was soon in demand as a popular preacher throughout northern Italy and southern France.

Before long, Anthony came to realize that, if he wanted to win human hearts—and hold them—as an inspiring preacher, he had to set time aside and nurture his own inner life and relationship with God.

SPECIAL PLACES WHERE ANTHONY SOUGHT GOD
In this chapter, I will introduce you to five places—hidden caves and hermitages—in central and northern Italy where Anthony

temporarily lived as a hermit and sought, before all else, a contemplative union with God.

THE HERMITAGE OF MONTE PAOLO

Two Franciscan friars from Bologna accompanied me by car in October 2006 to this hermitage, which sits about ten miles from the Italian town of Forlì mentioned above. This was an important starting point for Anthony.

Monte Paolo was Anthony's first real Franciscan residence in Italy. The Portuguese-born Anthony attended the Franciscan chapter near Assisi in 1221. Because he had not received an assignment at the chapter, the Franciscan provincial of Romagna invited Anthony to travel back with him to northern Italy and to celebrate Mass for four brothers living in the remote friary or hermitage of Monte Paolo.

This was the perfect hideaway or hermitage for Anthony after a failed missionary trip to Morocco and after ending up in Italy— thanks to his being blown badly off course in a storm during his intended return trip to Portugal.

When the two friars and I arrived at Monte Paolo, an elderly friar named Ludovico Bartolucci welcomed us and gave us a short history of the place. The rather large hermitage is not the same building where St. Anthony celebrated Mass for the four brothers. Back then, the hermitage of Monte Paolo was much simpler, according to Fr. Ludovico.

When Anthony first lived at the original hermitage at Monte Paolo, he discovered that one of the friars had built a cell in a cave nearby. And with this friar's approval, Anthony went out from the hermitage almost every day to pray in the cave and nurture his union with God. The little cave or grotto in the woods that Anthony used was later destroyed by landslides and floods, but in recent years it has been rebuilt on higher ground. Some of the stones of the original cave were used to rebuild the grotto, which many pilgrims visit today.

Fr. Ludovico said that Anthony lived at Monte Paolo for some ten months until the ordination at Forlì. This period became one of the most formative experiences of Anthony's life. Soon after his fellow Franciscans discovered how great a preacher and theologian he was, they stationed the saint at a friary in the prominent university town of Bologna. There Anthony taught theology to friars studying for the priesthood and had a convenient base for his evangelizing journeys.

A Grotto Near Monteluco Above Spoleto

Before we move on to this grotto, which we know was a favorite hideaway of St. Anthony, let me explain something by way of background. Once St. Anthony's preaching ministry took off in earnest, he saw all the more clearly that he needed to go away for periods of time, to pray in remote and solitary places to nurture his union with God. And this became even truer, no doubt, when as provincial minister of Romagna, between 1227 and 1230, he was serving his brothers. We don't know the exact dates when he visited the grotto at Monteluco, or *Le Celle di Cortona* or the cave at Mount La Verna. We simply know from historical evidence that he visited these places.

The grotto high above Spoleto is certainly an interesting case in point. Spoleto is a town about twenty-five miles south of Assisi. To reach this cavelike grotto in October of 2006, a friend and I had to take a half-hour taxi ride up a winding road that ascends the steep mountainside above Spoleto. The grotto is hidden away in what is still called the "Sacred Woods" (*Bosco Sacro*).

Even after we found this dark, awe-inspiring, and mystical woodland, it took us another half hour of searching before we found a little cave clearly marked as the grotto used by St. Anthony in the thirteenth century.

After offering brief prayers in the grotto, we took a few steps on a path that led out to a rocky ledge, overlooking the spectacular Spoleto Valley. Certainly, the early Franciscan hermits—St. Anthony and St. Francis included—who prayed on this and other mountains had a wonderful way of combining solitary prayer with awesome vistas that lift the human heart to songs of thanksgiving and praise!

LE CELLE DI CORTONA

Just outside Cortona, an Italian city about fifty miles northwest of Assisi, sits another hermitage popular with the early Franciscan friars. According to *Pilgrim's Companion to Franciscan Places,* St. Francis arrived here in 1211 "seeking a place of solitude." This book also mentions that Br. Elias, who worked on the Basilica of San Francesco in Assisi, likewise spent time here. It further notes that St. Anthony of Padua and St. Lawrence of Brindisi also came to Le Celle—both with a "strong propensity...to seek a more intense union with God."

Today, *Le Celle di Cortona* is basically a large hermitage and retreat center run by the Capuchin friars. A statue of St. Anthony stands in a prominent niche of the chapel. And behind the altar hangs a large painting depicting St. Francis of Assisi, St. Anthony of Padua, and St. Lawrence of Brindisi (a Capuchin saint who died in 1619).

The Capuchin friar affirmed his personal belief in the tradition that St. Anthony had come here to seek God in contemplation.

CAVE AT MOUNT LA VERNA

We know that St. Anthony had a special affection for Mount La Verna as a place for withdrawing to satisfy his contemplative yearnings. La Verna sits about ninety miles north of Assisi. St. Anthony certainly shared St. Francis' need for contemplative prayer as well as his love for the hidden caves of this special mountaintop retreat in northern Italy. Anthony loved praying in a little cave on Mount La Verna, not far from the rocky precipice where Francis was embraced by the fiery love of God when he received the stigmata, the five wounds of Christ.

In more recent times, Anthony's cave has been transformed into the Oratory of St. Anthony. Each week, hundreds of La Verna pilgrims stop and pray at Anthony's oratory, located atop the same rugged precipice as the Stigmata Chapel.

A Tree Hut in Camposampiero

As mentioned several times already, near the end of St. Anthony's life, he came to what was, no doubt, his favorite hideaway of all, the little house built into the branches of a tree in the town of Camposampiero. This is the town to which St. Anthony moved when he realized, after spending two very active years as a preacher in his beloved Padua, that his life was coming to an end.

Anthony sensed that he needed to take a break from his labors and to dedicate more time to God alone. In Camposampiero, a nobleman, Count Tiso, had earlier built a hermitage for friars seeking more time for contemplative prayer. Now, Anthony asked Tiso to construct a solitary hut in the branches of a large walnut tree in a forest, not far from the Franciscan hermitage where Anthony slept at night. Anthony spent a good part of the last weeks and months of his life praying in that small tree house.

It was my good fortune near the end of my trip from Assisi to Padua to spend my last four days with the Conventual Franciscan friars in their large friary attached to the magnificent Basilica of St. Anthony in Padua. One morning, a friar who lived there offered to drive me to Camposampiero so I could see where the walnut tree once stood.

Today, a quaint chapel stands over the place where St. Anthony's tree house was located. In this chapel, known as the Shrine of the Walnut Tree, there is a beautiful painting by Bonafacio de Pitata. It depicts Anthony preaching from the tree's branches to the faithful gathered below. Visitors approach this chapel by driving or walking down a lovely lane lined on each side by a long row of walnut trees.

Because of his great knowledge of Scripture, Anthony would have surely been aware of the symbolism of his spending his last months in a hut or cell built into the branches of a giant tree. And this symbolism was not lost on the artist who painted the picture of Anthony in the tree. The saint is shown in the tree halfway between heaven and earth. He has left his earthly concerns below in order to seek the face of God in holy contemplation and to share with the people his yearning to be with God in glory soon.

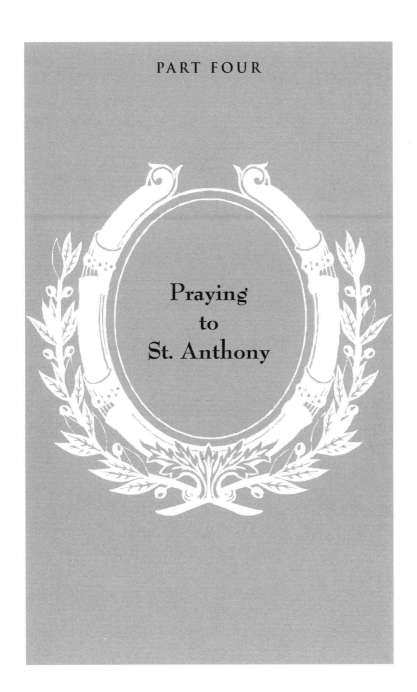

PART FOUR

Praying
to
St. Anthony

CHAPTER NINE

Finder, Teacher, Matchmaker, Guide

POPULAR CUSTOMS AND DEVOTIONS TO ST. ANTHONY

by Norman Perry, O.F.M.

I n the Basque region of Spain, St. Anthony of Padua is called Santo Casamentero, or the Holy Matchmaker. In 1668, when he had already been dead four hundred years, the Spanish government by royal order made him a soldier in its second infantry regiment. With each victory that regiment shared in, Anthony was promoted in rank. He was finally retired after reaching general in 1889. In many European countries, Anthony is the patron of sailors and fishermen. Everywhere his intercession is invoked for the return of lost and stolen things.

He is also regarded as a patron of priests and travelers, a protector against the devil, and a guardian of the mails. He is called the wonderworker and saint of the world.

The story and tradition of devotion to St. Anthony of Padua began almost with the moment of his death on June 13, 1231. His Franciscan brothers tried to keep his death secret to avoid violence and a struggle between citizens of Padua and Capodi Porte to claim his body for burial. Despite their efforts, children began running through the streets of Padua shouting, "The saint is dead!"

Crowds came to view the body of Anthony and attend his burial. His grave at once became a place of extraordinary devotion and numerous miracles. Legends would later attribute to him miracles worked even during his life.

Less than a month after his death the bishop, clergy, nobles and *podesta* (mayor) of Padua requested his canonization. They gave among their reasons the great veneration and miracles taking place at his tomb. Anthony was not yet dead a year when Pope Gregory IX declared him a saint of the Church, and construction began on a basilica to honor his memory and remains. A papal bull dated two days before the first anniversary of his death granted an indulgence of one year to all who would visit Anthony's tomb on his feast or within its octave.

Since then, popular piety and devotion to St. Anthony have taken many forms. In some cases, history offers a reason for a particular practice or form of devotion. In other cases, it explained by legend. And in some instances, the origin of the devotion may be lost or unexplained.

FINDER OF LOST OR STOLEN THINGS

Nearly everywhere, Anthony is asked to intercede with God for the return of things lost or stolen. Those who feel very familiar with him might pray, "Tony, Tony, turn around. Something's lost and must be found."

The reason for invoking St. Anthony's help in finding lost or stolen things is traced back to an incident in his own life. As the story goes, he had a book of psalms that was highly important to him. Besides the value of any book before the invention of printing, the psalter had the notes and comments he had made to use in teaching students in his Franciscan Order.

A novice who had already grown tired of living religious life decided to depart the community. Besides going AWOL, he also took Anthony's psalter! On realizing his psalter was missing, Anthony prayed that it would be found or returned to him. After his prayer the thieving novice was moved to return the psalter to him and to also return to the Order, which accepted him back.

Legend has embroidered this story a bit. The legend goes that the novice was stopped in his flight by a horrible devil brandishing an ax and threatening to trample him underfoot if he did not immediately return the book. Obviously a devil would hardly command anyone to do something good. But the core of the story would seem to be true. And the stolen book is said to be preserved in the Franciscan friary in Bologna.

In any event, shortly after his death people began praying through Anthony to find or recover lost and stolen articles. And the "Responsory of St. Anthony," composed by his contemporary, Julian of Spires, O.F.M., proclaims that "the sea obeys and fetters break / And lifeless limbs thou dost restore / While *treasures lost are found again* / When young or old thine aid implore."

THE NOVENA TO ST. ANTHONY

In many churches and at shrines the world over, it is common to find not only a statue of St. Anthony but also the existence of a continuing novena in honor of the saint. People drop in and out of the devotions, making novenas on nine or thirteen Tuesdays or Sundays. An obvious reason for Tuesday is that Anthony was buried on a Tuesday and that is when the miracles began.

The novena in honor of St. Anthony, according to one or more novena books and leaflets, is linked with a legend about a pious childless couple in Bologna around the year 1617. The story says has it that, after twenty-two years of longing for a child, the wife took her troubles to St. Anthony. He is said to have appeared to her in a dream, telling her, "For nine Tuesdays, one after the other, make visits to the church of my Order; on each of those days approach the holy sacraments of penance and of the altar, then pray before my picture, and what you ask, you shall obtain."

In one version of the story she conceived but gave birth to a badly deformed child. Again asking the saint's intercession, she took the child, at Anthony's instruction, to his altar, and the deformity at once disappeared.

Whatever fact may or may not be behind the legend, in 1898, Pope Leo XIII granted a plenary indulgence to those spending some time in devout meditation, prayers, or the performance of some other acts of piety in honor of St. Anthony of Padua on Tuesday or Sunday of any week with the intention of doing so for thirteen Tuesdays or Sundays without interruption. At the same time, Pope Leo XIII recommended the practice of St. Anthony bread.

ST. ANTHONY BREAD

Different legends or stories account for the donation of what is called St. Anthony bread. By at least one account it goes back to 1263, when it is said a child drowned near the Basilica of St. Anthony, which was still being built. His mother promised that if the child was restored to her she would give for the poor an amount of corn equal to the child's weight. Her prayer and promise were rewarded with the boy's return to life.

Another reason for the practice is traced back to a baker in France during 1890. Faced with a broken lock on the shop door, the baker prayed through St. Anthony that the locksmith could open the door without breaking it down. She promised bread for the poor in return for her favor. The door was opened, and she kept her promise.

Today St. Anthony bread is the offering or donation given to the poor in honor of St. Anthony for a favor received through his intercession. The donation could also go to a variety of charitable causes. In some places parents also make a gift for the poor after placing a newborn child under the protection of St. Anthony. It is a practice in some churches to bless small loaves of bread on the feast of St. Anthony and give them to those who want them.

ST. ANTHONY LILIES

In many places lilies are blessed on the feast of St. Anthony and given to those who want them. Some people dry them to preserve them or carry them on their person in a cloth container.

The lily is meant to remind the possessor of St. Anthony's purity and our own need to pray for the grace of purity in times of temptation.

This expression of piety is believed to have its roots in eighteenth-century France following the French Revolution. The Franciscans had been expelled from Corsica and their church abandoned. Yet people came to the church for an annual observance of the feast of St. Anthony on June 13. One year, some months after Anthony's feast, a man wandered into the church and found lilies from the celebration still fresh.

The custom of blessing lilies is another of those approved by Pope Leo XIII. The prayer of blessing asks for the grace to preserve chastity, peace, and protection against the evil one.

ST. ANTHONY'S BRIEF

"Behold the Cross of the Lord! Be gone, you enemy powers! The lion of the tribe of Juda, the root of David has conquered! Alleluia!" are words that Pope Sixtus V had inscribed on the obelisk he erected in the quadrangle in front of St. Peter's Basilica in Rome. They are also words attributed to St. Anthony known as the Brief (or letter) of St. Anthony. Some people carry the words with them, a form of asking for protection against the devil.

The custom of carrying and praying the words comes from the story of a woman in Portugal tempted by the devil and obsessed with thoughts of suicide. As the story is related, she was on her way to drown herself but stopped off at a Franciscan chapel to pray before a statue of St. Anthony. During her prayer she fell asleep and saw St. Anthony, who released her from her disturbed state of mind. When she woke up she found a letter, or brief, given to her by St. Anthony, with the words quoted above. It has been written that the original letter was preserved with the crown jewels of Portugal. This practice may also be rooted in a story about Anthony's own struggle with the devil, who was trying to choke him. Anthony, says the early account by a contemporary friar, put the devil to flight by invoking Mary's help and making the sign of the cross.

GUARDIAN OF THE MAIL

Perhaps you've received a letter with the initials *S.A.G.* written somewhere on the envelope or under the flap or stamp. Or you may even have received a letter with a stamp bearing a picture of St. Anthony with the letters *S.A.G.* The letters stand for *St. Anthony Guide* or *Guard*. Usually the stamp has no more postal value than a Christmas or Easter seal. But in 1931, for the seventh centenary of Anthony's death, both Italy and Portugal issued postage stamps in his honor.

St. Anthony's association with the mail is said to have come from an incident in his life. According to a story in Charles Warren Stoddard's *St. Anthony: Wonder-Worker of Padua*, Anthony wished to journey to the town of Campo San Pietro, some distance from where he was staying. The purpose of the trip was to rest and reflect. He dutifully wrote a letter to his superior to ask permission for the trip. But when it came time to give the letter to a messenger, it could not be found. Anthony took it as a sign that he was not to go and put the trip from his mind. Inexplicably, some time later he received an answer from the superior giving permission for the trip.

A further association with the mail goes back to an event that was said to have happened in 1792. One Antonio Dante, so the story goes, journeyed to Lima, Peru, leaving his wife behind in

Spain. After his departure she wrote to him many times without receiving any reply. Finally, she went to the church of St. Francis in Oviedo and placed in the hands of St. Anthony's statue a letter to her husband in Peru. She prayed that Anthony would get the letter to him and obtain a reply.

According to the tale, she returned to the chapel the next day. A letter was still clasped in the hands of the statue. She began scolding St. Anthony for not delivering her letter. The noise she made prompted the sacristan, who said he had tried to get the letter from Anthony's hands but without success. The wife is then supposed to have reached up and taken the letter from Anthony's hands quite easily. At the same time, three hundred gold coins spilled from the statue's sleeve. When the letter was opened, it was not the wife's letter but a letter from the husband. He said that, not hearing from her for so long, he had thought her dead. But her most recent letter had been delivered by a Franciscan priest.

HOLY MATCHMAKER

As mentioned earlier, among the Basques St. Anthony is called Santo Casamentero, the Holy Matchmaker or saint of those looking for husbands. According to the *Handbook of Christian Feasts and Customs* by Rev. Francis X. Weiser, Basque girls make a pilgrimage to his shrine in Durango on Anthony's feast. They pray that he will help them find "a good boy."

It may help that the young men are said to make the same journey to the shrine, where, gathered outside the church until the young women are finished with their prayers, they wait to ask them to dance.

Weiser speculates that the association with engagement and marriage is inspired by all the statues and pictures of Anthony carrying the infant Jesus in his arms.

St. Anthony and the Child Jesus

St. Anthony has been pictured by artists and sculptors in all kinds of ways. He is depicted with a book in his hands, or with a lily or a torch. He has been painted preaching to fish, holding a monstrance with the Blessed Sacrament in front of a mule, or preaching in the public square or from a nut tree.

But since the seventeenth century we most often find the saint shown with the child Jesus in his arms or even with the child standing on a book the saint holds. A fuller treatment of this popular image of St. Anthony is found in the previous chapter.

The Chaplet of St. Anthony

Curious readers occasionally share descriptions or drawings of a chaplet of thirteen beads with a medal of St. Anthony. They want to know what kind of rosary or crown this may be. The beads are called the Chaplet of St. Anthony. The chaplet is prayed by saying, in each set, an Our Father on the first bead, a Hail Mary on the second, and a Glory Be on the third. The chaplet seems to have had its origin in nineteenth-century Padua.

Patron of Sailors, Travelers, and Fishermen

In Portugal, Italy, France, and Spain, St. Anthony is the patron saint of sailors and fishermen. According to Fr. Weiser, his statue is sometimes placed in a shrine on the ship's mast. And the sailors sometimes scold him if he doesn't respond quickly enough to their prayers.

Not only those who travel the seas but also other travelers and vacationers pray that they may be kept safe through Anthony's intercession.

Several stories and legends may account for associating the saint with travelers and sailors.

First, there is the very real fact of Anthony's own travels in preaching the gospel, particularly his journey and mission to preach the gospel in Morocco, a mission cut short by severe illness. But after his recovery and return to Europe, he was a man always on the go, heralding the Good News.

There is also a story of two Franciscan sisters who wished to make a pilgrimage to a shrine of our Lady, but they did not know the way. A young man is supposed to have volunteered to guide them. On their return from the pilgrimage, one of the sisters announced that it was her patron saint, Anthony, who had guided them.

Still another story says that, in 1647, Fr. Erastius Villani of Padua was returning by ship to Italy from Amsterdam. The ship, with its crew and passengers, was caught in a violent storm. All seemed doomed. Fr. Erastius encouraged everyone to pray to St. Anthony. Then he threw into the heaving seas some pieces of cloth that had touched a relic of St. Anthony. At once, the storm ended, the winds stopped, and the sea became calm.

TEACHER, PREACHER, DOCTOR OF THE SCRIPTURES

Among the Franciscans themselves and in the liturgy of his feast, St. Anthony is celebrated as a teacher and preacher extraordinaire. He was the first teacher in the Franciscan Order to be given the special approval and blessing of St. Francis to instruct his brother Franciscans. His effectiveness in calling people back to the faith through his preaching resulted in the title "Hammer of Heretics." Just as important were his peacemaking and calls for justice.

In canonizing Anthony in 1232, Pope Gregory IX spoke of him as the "Ark of the Testament" and the "Repository of Holy Scripture." That explains why St. Anthony is frequently pictured with a burning light or a book of the Scriptures in his hands. In 1946, Pope Pius XII officially declared Anthony a Doctor of the Church. It is in Anthony's love of the word of God and his prayerful efforts to understand and apply it to the situations of everyday life that the Church especially wants us to imitate St. Anthony. While noting in the prayer of his feast the effectiveness that Anthony is known for as an intercessor, the Church especially wants us to learn from Anthony the teacher the meaning of true wisdom and what it means to become like Jesus, who humbled and emptied himself for our sakes and went about doing good.

CHAPTER TEN

A Guided Tour in Anthony's Footsteps
FROM LISBON TO PADUA
by Carol Ann Morrow

The saints ask us that we follow in their footsteps toward the One who inspired them. And sometimes, walking literally in their footsteps can help us understand not only their journey but also our own.

So, given the invitation and the opportunity to travel with Franciscan friar Jim Bok and thirty other men and women of faith who also felt called to the journey, I said, "yes, yes, yes." I traveled to Portugal and Italy in the year of the eight hundredth anniversary of Anthony's birth and entered as fully as I could into the mind and heart of the man now known as Anthony of Padua. Five years later, during the millennium year 2000, I repeated the journey, once again with Fr. Jim Bok and forty-three other pilgrims. On the second journey, I was able to enlarge my capacity for appreciating Anthony still more.

LISBON, ANTHONY'S BIRTHPLACE
It's a bit startling to realize that Anthony is not Italian but Portuguese. But beginning a pilgrimage in Lisbon ensures that I will never forget how far, how long, how adventurous a journey was the life of Anthony, born Fernando Bulhom in Lisbon, Portugal.

In 1195, the year of his birth, Lisbon was not Portugal's capital. Portugal had defined its borders only fifty years earlier and now was still defending those borders from the Moors of North Africa.

We pilgrims couldn't see all the landmarks familiar to Anthony because on November 1, 1755, what the Portuguese call the Great Earthquake destroyed many of them. Still, today's Lisbon perches on the same steep hills, overlooking the same Tagus River, the largest river on the Iberian Peninsula. Now it is spanned by graceful bridges, filled with large ships and small sailing boats and admired by tourists. We admired it because we imagined Fernando looking out at that same powerful current and feeling drawn to adventure and exploration.

When he looked up, he saw the Castle of St. George, the residence of the earliest Portuguese royalty. I can imagine little Fernando scrambling up the steep hill to the castle's edge to gain perspective on the river and on his own neighborhood, the Alfama. We did.

In Fernando's day, the Alfama was Lisbon's oldest and most prestigious neighborhood. Its streets are still the narrow, twisting labyrinth they were when the saint was a boy. Tour books compare it to the Casbah.

In open-air patios or in tiny taverns and neighborhood restaurants, it is easy to taste the cuisine Anthony may have eaten: fish, to be certain, especially dried, salted cod (bacalhau). I tried it, attempting to commune with Fernando's childhood menu. Luckily, it's not required of Anthony's pilgrims that we eat it every day as Portuguese sailors had to.

In this maze are three key places in the life of Anthony: his birthplace, the cathedral where he was baptized (and where he attended the cathedral school), and the monastery that he entered to become an Augustinian canon. None of these is the original structure, but at least the last two are in the same location as they were in the saint's youth.

Pope John Paul II has visited and prayed at the site where Fernando Bulhom was born, a little niche beneath Santo António à Sé, a church built in Anthony's honor. The stone walls of that tiny undercroft bear hundreds of written endearments and thanksgiving to the saint, a kind of holy graffiti in a host of languages. The present church, built in 1812, was financed by alms collected by the children of Lisbon.

We learned how much children love St. Anthony. He is often called *Antoninho* (Little Anthony) there, and it seems that the children, also diminutive, identify with him. As pilgrims, we tried to become like children ourselves as we followed the path of Antoninho. Having come straight to this church from the airport, we celebrated Mass, in thanksgiving for our arrival, at the place that marks the beginning of Anthony's journey—his birth. The image of Anthony above the main altar was distinctly Portuguese. The day of our visit was September 8, feast of Mary's birth, so our day emphasized births, beginnings, and the rebirth that pilgrims seek.

Later we lit votives to add to the many already flickering beneath a painting of the saint. Petitions and thanksgivings are tucked into the picture's frame. Flowers are crammed in generous bouquets in a pail in front of this image. In this very first city, it was already quite clear how loved was the saint in whose steps we were following.

The cathedral (*Sé*) of Lisbon is just a block from Anthony's home. In fact, one can see its twin towers from the courtyard of Santo António. It looks like a fortress. The baptismal font, said to be the original, is in an alcove to the left inside the main entrance. Today, this alcove is lined with the distinctive blue tiles (*azulejos*) particular to Portugal. These depict the story of Anthony preaching to the fish. The cathedral itself is new, though legend says that a cross recessed into the stone of a stairway to the right of the entrance was drawn there by the finger of Fernando.

We drove past São Vincente de Fora, or St. Vincent's Outside the Walls, which is a considerable distance from these first two churches. The current white limestone Italianate buildings are new, but it was to St. Vincent's on this same site that Fernando came around 1210 to become a canon of St. Augustine. Here, the young man began to develop not only his considerable intellect but also a tremendous thirst to know God. That thirst led him to leave Lisbon for a more austere and secluded life in Coimbra.

SEEKING SILENCE IN COIMBRA

Coimbra is also on the water, as our group discovered, but it was not the Rio Mondego that drew Anthony. In 1212 he requested a move to the Convent (monastery) of Santa Cruz in Coimbra, the principal house of the Portuguese Augustinians, because he wanted knowledge and wanted silence. He hoped to find them both in Coimbra, Portugal's foremost center of learning then—and home to a fine university today. Santa Cruz Monastery was known to have a well-stocked library and excellent teachers.

The old town of Coimbra still exists, its steep and narrow streets tangled much like Lisbon's Alfama. The church of Santa Cruz is open and active, but the monastery remains only in remnants— pieces from two different eras, including Anthony's day. It is open to visitors, many of whom want to see the tombs of Portugal's first two kings, Afonso and Sancho. We simply want to be where Anthony lived—and where he decided to become a Franciscan.

The relics of the first Franciscan martyrs—Berard, Peter, Adjutus, Accursius and Otto—were brought to Santa Cruz while Anthony was in residence. Relics gave a church more stature, and Pedro, son of King Sancho, used his influence to have these prestigious remains brought to Coimbra, where he lived and worshiped. We had been expecting to see relics of some size—after all, there were five friars. The remains of the five martyred friars, however, are now contained within two rather small (friar-shaped) reliquaries, made of silver.

I'd seen illustrations in which the battered bodies of the friars were dramatically carried to Coimbra's monastery door. On reflection, we knew that couldn't be true, since they had been martyred in Morocco and their bodies returned (by whom, one wonders) to the port of Lisbon or possibly up the Atlantic coast to a smaller port nearer Coimbra. Then, overland transport would still be necessary, since the city is more than fifty miles from the coast.

Those are the practicalities that we pilgrims pondered. In any case, the impact of those five Franciscan lives—and deaths—on Fernando was life-changing. We knew this. His welcoming these martyrs' remains became for him a challenge to his way of life. Should he remain a canon of St. Augustine—or should he leave the safety of the cloister to become a martyr himself?

We did not locate the little church dedicated to St. Anthony of Egypt (the *first* St. Anthony), but we knew that it was near Coimbra and that it was home to poor men following the path of St. Francis. Like their founder, they had little and begged alms from others. We could picture them making their way to the substantial entryway of Santa Cruz Monastery. When they knocked, the young Augustinian, already moved by their brother martyrs, answered the door. He felt it as a summons. He decided to become a Franciscan and, he hoped, a martyr as well.

This change didn't happen in a day, but by the end of that year, 1220, Fernando had become a friar, taken a new name—after Anthony of Egypt—and sailed from his homeland to preach the gospel in the same country where the first Franciscans had met their deaths. He never returned to the land of his birth.

IMAGINE MOROCCO AND SICILY

Friar Anthony never set foot in Morocco—and neither did we. But Anthony tried! He sailed across the Mediterranean to the Moroccan coast, but many speculate that he became ill on the voyage, because he never fulfilled his dream of preaching the gospel to the Moors.

Since the southern border of Portugal had fluctuated often in its inception—sometimes the land belonged to the Moors, sometimes not—we speculated that Anthony felt a special affinity for Morocco and its people.

The new missionary was so ill that it seemed imperative to return him to Portugal. But unseasonable weather prevented the ship's regaining the Straits of Gibraltar. The Mediterranean spit them out like seaweed at the Straits of Messina instead, on the island of Sicily. We tender tourists were spared this harrowing part of Anthony's life journey.

FRANCIS DRAWS ANTHONY LIKE A MAGNET

On both visits, we pilgrims flew from Lisbon to Rome, so we were pampered once again in ways that Anthony, centuries earlier, could not have even imagined. Nor could we imagine how he walked halfway up the length of Italy to the valley of Umbria (northeast of Rome), where the followers of Francis were gathering for a general meeting, or chapter, in May 1221. For Anthony, it had to have been a genuinely new chapter, with unfamiliar people speaking an unfamiliar language.

Three thousand friars gathered in the woods near St. Mary of the Angels to discuss a revision of their rule, or way of life. We know that Francis wasn't well during this time—and some biographers doubt that Anthony ever regained his health, although his stamina will become apparent as we continue to trace his journey.

While we traveled somewhat logically from Rome to Assisi to Padua, that is no adequate measure of Anthony's travels, I must confess at once. What we know of his whereabouts began in Assisi in 1221, moved north and westward to other Italian towns and cities, and then took him by foot to the south of France from 1224 to 1227. The intrepid traveler returned to Italy and, at least once, traveled south to Rome. We know that, by 1228, he was in Padua.

We had in our pilgrim's progress about as many days remaining as he had years. Obviously, our pilgrimage required an economy of choices.

So, I will recount our journey as though we were moving in the order Anthony did. We are attempting to trace his life journey, but we shuffled the order—and added places where we knew St. Francis had been. This disclaimer is issued in the event that you try to follow in *our* footsteps!

ADOPTED INTO ITALY

St. Mary of the Angels is in the Umbrian Valley. Assisi is the ascent beyond. We began in the valley as Anthony did.

St. Mary of the Angels is a large church built to house a small chapel, the Portiuncula, where Anthony seems certain to have prayed. Fewer than half our group could fit into the tiny space at once, and we were not the only pilgrims eager to kneel where Francis and his followers have knelt. But we all managed to steal some silent moments

The interior is so roughly finished that the very bricks and mortar that Francis put in place when he repaired the tiny chapel must surely be exposed. For many of us, it was a favored place to which we returned often during our time in the Assisi area.

After the friars concluded their gathering in 1221, the young refugee—who was, so to speak, without portfolio—asked a friar to receive him into the province of Upper Italy. Anthony was pleased to live a quiet life in Monte Paolo. Although he was humble, at an ordination in Forli his intelligence, education, and oratorical gifts were discovered, and he was asked to become a traveling preacher. We have our own friar-preacher with us to answer our questions and celebrate Eucharist with us as we pursue our journey.

Anthony's role was to counsel Catholics and strengthen their faith despite the influence of various heretical movements afoot in Europe at the time. In 1223 Francis engaged Anthony to teach the friars so that they too could help the faithful discern the gospel way to live in those chaotic times. He is said to have taught in Bologna, at its university, among other places. To us, Anthony's life-style sounded like that of a mission preacher.

In 1227, Anthony was appointed head of the province of friars in Upper Italy. So he returned there, never to leave Italy again.

ANTHONY VISITS ROME

In 1228, Anthony was invited by Gregory IX, a great friend of the Franciscans, to preach to the papal curia and Easter pilgrims at St. John Lateran in Rome. When we were in Rome ourselves, we visited this church with its links to Franciscan history. It is also the parish church of the bishop of Rome, the Holy Father. We learned that St. John Lateran is where Francis, with his first eleven followers, went to ask for the pope's blessing on his fledgling community.

In the mosaic in the apse of the church, Mary (with a miniature Pope Nicholas IV at her side) and Sts. Peter, Paul, John the Evangelist, John the Baptist, and Andrew are joined by the much later Francis and Anthony, two-thirds the size of the others.

Anthony paid a second visit here in 1230, conferring with Pope Gregory about the Franciscan rule, which required approval from the pope. Anthony was part of the delegation representing the friars' concerns, because he was a great thinker and also a man who lived and loved the way of life that Francis had begun. It is this combination that commands our respect, which grows as we travel on the path Anthony once took.

While we were in Rome, we attended the weekly open-air Mass celebrated in front of St. Peter's Basilica. The celebrant was Pope John Paul II. We were visiting the pope of our day, as Anthony visited the pope of his. We also paid homage at the simple tomb of Pope John XXIII, in a basement niche at St. Peter's.

ANTHONY AND PADUA FINALLY CONNECT

Anthony and Padua are so tightly linked in the Catholic mind that whenever we speak of the saint, this Italian town is invoked as well (except in Portugal, where he is known as St. Anthony of Lisbon). It's uncertain when Anthony made Padua his home, but it was probably toward the end of 1228. At most, the Franciscan preacher lived there for a period less than three years! We pilgrims, in contrast, had about *three days* to discover what won the saint's heart in this fair city.

Padua has had a university since 1222. Anthony probably liked the feel of a city that respected scholarship. We walked through one of the city's original gates. Looking up at the rounded stone arch, we could imagine that Anthony did so hundreds of years before us. It seems likely, since beyond this gate is the main plaza of the old city.

Anthony was an inveterate and popular preacher in Padua and attracted crowds too large for any church. His voice may have reached listeners who stood at the same windows from which residents now hang their laundry.

In fact, laundry was hanging from iron-railed balconies to catch the breeze and dry in the sun, just as it did in 1228. On other balconies, bright red flowers soak up the sun. We too soaked up some sunshine, and we attempted to soak up the aura of Anthony as well.

The Basilica of St. Anthony was, of course, never imagined by Anthony. It was begun just a year after his death, a tribute to the strong affection of Paduans during the life of the man they call *il Santo.* (Other saints require additional ID!) It is the third-most visited European destination for European pilgrims, after Rome and Lourdes. In the year of my first visit, because it was the eighth centenary of Anthony's birth, *eight million* visitors came to pray in this cavernous basilica.

We joined them in faith and devotion, moved to be part of a spiritual energy that permeated the majestic structure. The basilica is said to be inspired in some ways by St. Mark's in Venice, which we also visited, but it is simpler in many respects, perhaps because it is unified around a simple friar.

That's not to say it's simple. It has pointed minaret-like towers, rounded towers with rounded rooflines, and a Gothic interior that is a bit dark. We enter in a hush and can tell by the crowds where the Chapel of St. Anthony is. This niche was redesigned during the Renaissance, and its walls are white marble bas-reliefs showing scenes of Anthony's life. I'm describing, though, what I noticed in succeeding visits, because, like all Catholic pilgrims to Padua, we were being drawn instead to the tomb of the saint.

A guard had to move us along with cries of *Avanti* ("move on") as we have our moment to touch the length of the tomb in which Anthony's bones now rest. The black marble of the Titian-designed tomb is rough and worn from the affectionate touches of people like us—who have been helped by Anthony in times of need. Fr. Jim has been carrying a thick packet of prayers and petitions from friends of the friars in the United States. This is that packet's final destination.

The packet rests alongside a leg brace, a soccer ball, fresh bouquets, and framed infant clothes with baby pictures included, plus silver and gold images of feet, legs, lungs, and torsos. These are called *ex votos,* a term derived from the Latin for "from a vow." They are brought to the tomb in fulfillment of a promise (vow) made in return for the saint's able assistance. I for one had not appreciated the scope of the saint's apparent influence with the Almighty.

We bustled to the Chapel of the Treasury, where many more *ex votos* hang on either side of the relics (the treasures) of Anthony: his incorrupt tongue, his jaw, his vocal cords. Personally, I was more moved by the *ex votos*, but it does amaze that the physical attributes that enabled Anthony to preach the word, in both Italy and France, to popes and peasants, to his brothers and to political leaders, are the parts miraculously preserved for our veneration.

We all resolve to return again on a weekday (which will be possible—and is a good idea), because the Sunday crowds nearly crush us at times.

VIA DEL SANTO

While the Basilica is the apex of our pilgrimage, it is not its end. It cannot be, because it is not where the saint met his end. That is why there is a simple road—Via del Santo, the Way of the Saint—which leads to Camposampiero.

In 1231, Anthony was tired—and some of his weariness was due to illness. He was so selfless a preacher and confessor that, in the preceding Lent, he had exhausted himself in a marathon of daily sermons that inspired many Paduans to seek him out to receive absolution and advice.

It seemed to us that the saint who had longed for solitude at Monte Paolo (and also at La Verna, where Francis loved to pray) surely found it in this small town with its small chapel. The chapel is on the site of the long-gone walnut tree, where Anthony's friend, Count Tiso, built a sort-of tree house for the popular saint, so that he could have the silence and seclusion he was seeking. That seems a desperate move, but, if the crowds were anything close in number and vitality to what we had experienced in the basilica, not so far-fetched a notion!

A community of Poor Clares, the contemplative order begun by Sts. Clare and Francis, live in Camposampiero, and they pray the Divine Hours in this chapel. Our guide says that walnut trees typically flower in April, but those at Camposampiero blossom in June "because they are St. Anthony's." Since we are there in fall, we cannot test the truth of this testimony.

We leave the little chapel to visit the parish church. This building is constructed around the room in Count Tiso's home where Anthony slept. This is the modest cell where Anthony had a consoling vision of the Infant Jesus. We would never have known about it except that Count Tiso saw such a light that he thought Anthony's room was on fire and he flung open the door. The saint swore his friend to secrecy, but after Anthony's death Tiso felt free to speak of the vision he had also shared.

We begin our return to Padua, which is where Anthony wanted to go when he felt death coming. He got to Arcella (where he had been confessor to another community of Poor Clares), but his body gave out and he had to ask the friars who were transporting him in a cart to let him rest there.

Today's Arcella is actually a suburb of modern Padua, which has grown to embrace it. But in 1231, it was too far away for Anthony to reach. So he asked the friars to hold him up so he could *see* the city he so loved. He blessed it before he died, shortly after the feast of Pentecost, on June 13, 1231.

Because Arcella's church is the hub of an active parish community, it is a busy place. We have just a few moments before Mass begins to circle the shrine of the saint who died there. We learn the story that when he died, the little children of Padua intuitively felt the loss of a kind and holy man. They came out of their homes, crying in the streets, "The holy father is dead!"

But he isn't really.

Twice, I've had the opportunity to follow Anthony of Padua around, sensing the spiritual energy his holiness still generates hundreds of years later. I've heard the people with whom I traveled tell their stories of how Anthony interceded for them, inspired them, and supported them. I've had occasion to remember and rejoice in his role in my own life.

At the beginning of our journey, we saw, over the baptismal font where the infant Fernando had been baptized, these words: "The whole world rejoices in his light." As pilgrims, we had traced that light. Fr. Bok, our Franciscan chaplain, summed up our pilgrimage experience: "We are not going home as great theologians, but we can be little people giving off a big light." That's enough reason to seek out this saint—in prayer and in pilgrimage. I highly recommend it!

CHAPTER ELEVEN

Praying to St. Anthony

M any Church historians and other observers of religious trends would say that prayer and devotion to the saints declined in popularity in the years following Vatican II (1962–1965). This was certainly true in some sectors of the Church. To some extent, the decline even affected such a popular Catholic saint as Anthony of Padua. In a good number of churches, however, especially where the Tuesday novenas to St. Anthony were popular in the past, that popularity has continued as strong as ever. This is particularly true of the novenas before Anthony's feast, June 13.

It would not be fair to claim, however, that the Second Vatican Council encouraged the faithful to abandon the popular practice of prayer and devotion to the saints. It was more a matter of emphasis and of looking carefully at priorities in Catholic teaching. The Council reminded Catholics that the central focus of the Church's prayer life and worship is the Eucharist, which is a celebration of Christ's saving action among us. The Eucharist is not one of many equal devotions in the Church. It is the summit of Catholic prayer and worship.

Churches built with this realization have sometimes led to an almost obsessive concern that everything in the building focus on the altar. In some churches statues of the saints have been removed, or at least their numbers reduced. Vatican II gave no orders to remove images. In fact in its *Constitution on the Sacred Liturgy,* it clearly gave this instruction: "The practice of placing sacred images in churches so that they may be venerated is to be firmly maintained. Nevertheless," the document adds, "their number should be moderate and their relative locations should reflect right order. Otherwise they may create confusion among the Christian people and promote a faulty sense of devotion" (*Sacrosanctum Concilium,* 125).

There was no set determination on the part of the Church to lead people away from praying or showing devotion to the saints. Rather, the Church sought to place a healthy emphasis on the centrality of Jesus. This may have led to a lessening of attention paid to the saints, including even Mary, at least in some sectors of the Church.

It is human and understandable if we sometimes blame Vatican II for whatever we do not like about the Church today. But there is nothing in the Council documents that downgrades devotion to the saints. It does, however, give us admonitions and guidance, as when it says, "Let the faithful remember, moreover, that true devotion consists neither in sterile or transitory affection, nor in a certain vain credulity, but proceeds from true faith" (*Lumen Gentium,* 67).

In *Lumen Gentium,* the pope and bishops said that when we look at the lives of those who have faithfully followed Christ, we are inspired to seek

> the City that is to come.... In the lives of those who, sharing in our humanity, are however more perfectly transformed into the image of Christ, God vividly manifests His presence and His face to men.... Nor is it by the title of example only that we cherish the memory of those in heaven, but still more in order that the union of the whole Church may be strengthened in the Spirit by the practice of fraternal charity. For just as Christian communion among wayfarers

brings us closer to Christ, so our companionship with the saints joins us to Christ.... It is supremely fitting, therefore, that we love those friends and coheirs of Jesus Christ, who are also our brothers and extraordinary benefactors, that we render due thanks to God for them. (*Lumen Gentium*, 50)

The Church has not for a moment relinquished its belief in "the communion of saints" as professed in the Apostles' Creed. An Episcopalian sculptor, highly respected for his thoughtful renditions of well-known saints, was once asked by a Roman Catholic if he believed in praying to the saints, since some non-Catholics are known to be critical of the practice of praying to the saints. The artist answered, "We often ask our friends who are still alive to pray for us. Why should we not ask our good brothers and sisters who have died and are in the presence of God to pray for us?"

If people turned to Anthony for help and guidance when he walked this earth, why should the faithful today not be encouraged to seek St. Anthony's help now while he shares fullness of life with the risen Christ in heaven? Do we believe, or do we not, what we profess in the Apostles' Creed: that in Christ we form one communion of love not only with our fellow believers here on earth but with those already sharing God's life in heaven?

It is a venerable Christian tradition to turn in prayer to St. Anthony—and to other saintly men and women already enjoying the glorious presence of God. Of course, we are encouraged to pray to St. Anthony and to God in our own words. At times, however, you may find it convenient to use prayers that are addressed to St. Anthony and already in popular use. The following seven prayers to him are related to specific circumstances and needs. You may find them helpful in your personal devotion to the saint.

Special Prayers to St. Anthony

Prayer to Find What Is Lost

Since your death, St. Anthony, the Lord has worked countless wonders and answered the prayers of countless people because of your loving prayer for them. Those who have experienced the power of prayer offered through you have told how God was pleased to help them in their need, restoring peace of mind, healing the sick, or finding what was lost, spiritual or material. Now in our need we ask you to pray for each of us that we might continue to share in God's loving care and protection and through you be drawn to eternal life. Amen.

Prayer to St. Anthony Holding the Child Jesus

Blessed Anthony, Jesus was the center of your life. It must be the same for me, as for every Christian. Your purity of soul, your humility, your simple radiant faith fits well with the gentle and humble Savior, who was a little child to his Father in heaven. Help us to give up our desire for power and control. Keep us from a merely intellectual faith, and may we be totally dependent on Jesus as you were, with the helplessness of a little child. Amen.

Prayer to St. Anthony Holding the Bible

Blessed Anthony, the Lord made the Scriptures a glowing flame in your mind and heart. Your sermons were filled with the words of the Lord. With the same reverent openness as you had, may we listen to the same Lord speaking to us in the Bible. May we feel the presence of Jesus in the Scriptures, just like the people of your day when you preached that Word to them. Amen.

Prayer to St. Anthony with the Burning Flame

St. Anthony, we marvel at your enthusiasm, especially in your years of preaching. Your hours of prayer set you on fire to use your great talent in tireless preaching, even though it damaged your health in your last days. May our devotion to you awaken our cold hearts, sated with the creature comforts and distractions of our day. May the presence of Jesus in our prayer warm us to genuine love for others. Give us the courage and ardor to stand for the truth, whatever the cost. Amen.

Prayer to St. Anthony Holding a Lily

St. Anthony, you were truly spoken of by Jesus when he said, "Blessed are the pure of heart, the single-minded." Your faith and love of Jesus led you to respect and honor God's beautiful creation, our bodies, made in the image of Jesus. Your mind and heart were free of all double-dealing with God and with your brothers and sisters. His love shone through you as through crystals. Help us also to be pure of heart and mind, with wholehearted love of God. Amen.

Prayer to St. Anthony Holding a Cross

St. Anthony, before sinners and saints you raised the cross to give us courage in suffering, to be our only hope of salvation, and to be a sign of the price God paid to show us his love. You always preached penance—a turning away from anyone and anything that separates us from God, even slightly. You put the First Thing first—the dying of Jesus, given to us that we might enter into his spirit as he died—and his Resurrection, which he wills to share with us. Help us to die to sin, large and small, and by this dying to be lifted up in grace, once and for all, as we die many times throughout our days. Amen.

Prayer to St. Anthony, Instrument of Justice and Peace

St. Anthony, during your life you imitated St. Francis of Assisi in his love for gospel poverty and the poor. While you desired little for yourself, you were constantly alive to the needs of the poor and little people of the world. You shared what you had with them and demanded justice for them. We ask now, in your name, that we may not be overly desirous of wealth or possessions. May we share what we have with others less fortunate. Make us always instruments and voices for peace and justice in our world. Amen.

CHAPTER TWELVE

Making a Novena to St. Anthony

Perhaps the most popular way of showing devotion to St. Anthony is by making a novena. Typically, those who seek Anthony's help make a novena of nine or thirteen Tuesdays or nine or thirteen consecutive days of prayer, public or private. They do this for a variety of personal intentions (to ask for the healing of a loved one, for example, or to find a lost wedding ring or a better relationship with God). Tuesday is an especially popular day for praying the novena to St. Anthony because his burial day, June 17, 1231, fell on a Tuesday.

Novenas originally began in Spain and France as preparation for the feast of Christmas. The Latin word *novena* means nine, and that number was chosen to represent the nine months Jesus lived in the womb of his mother. Later, the practice spread to the feasts of Mary and the saints.

Some people see novenas as bordering on the superstitious because their efficacy seems to be based on the number nine, as if it had magical power. Such superstitious attitudes, of course, must be guarded against and avoided. A prayer's efficacy is not based on our reciting a prayer *nine* or *thirteen times* but on our earnestness and perseverance, on our trust in God and confidence in Mary or other saints such as Anthony of Padua.

PERSEVERANCE IS THE KEY

Holding oneself to the discipline of repeating a prayerful request for a set number of days manifests personal perseverance and trust, which in turn reveal the petitioner's earnestness and fervor.

We are reminded of Jesus' parable about the persistent individual who comes to a friend's house at midnight and asks for three loaves of bread. The friend says, "Don't bother me. I'm already in bed." Jesus points out that if the petitioner fails to motivate the friend to get out of bed and share bread because of friendship, he will likely do so because of his persistence. Jesus is teaching us, therefore, that we should persist, or persevere, in prayer (see Luke 11:5-9).

There is more than one way to construct a novena to St. Anthony. If you were to visit different St. Anthony shrines around this country or around the world, you might find that novenas to him take different forms and include different prayers. We offer the following format as one good way to proceed.

There is one popular prayer that is included in novenas to St. Anthony quite often: the *Si Quaeris Miracula*. This ancient prayer or hymn goes back to approximately 1235, or a few short years after Anthony's death. Because of its ancient character, linking us almost to the time of Anthony himself, it is highly revered. Often referred to as the "Responsory of St. Anthony," it was written in Latin by Julian of Speyer, a Franciscan friar with German roots, who died in Paris around 1250. Composed as part of the Divine Office for St. Anthony's feast day, the prayer takes the title *Si Quaeris Miracula* ("If you ask for miracles") from its first words.

It's not easy to find a satisfying English translation, so most churches or shrines prefer to go with the old and venerable English wording, as we do below. Despite the odd phrasing, most devotees of St. Anthony seem to like the familiar ring of the lines. The prayer is basically a listing of all the favors, healings, and wonders attributed to Anthony almost from the moment of his death in 1231. It is also a celebration of Anthony's intercessory power and of the overflowing goodness of God.

A Novena to St. Anthony of Padua
(with daily reflections based on Anthony's sermons)
Responsory and Prayers

THE RESPONSORY OF ST. ANTHONY (*Si Quaeris Miracula...*)
If you ask for miracles,
Death, error, all calamities,
The leprosy and demons fly,
And health succeeds infirmities.

The sea obeys and fetters break,
And lifeless limbs thou dost restore;
Whilst treasures lost are found again
When young or old thine aid implore.

All dangers vanish at thy prayer,
And direst need doth quickly flee.
Let those who know thy power
Proclaim—
Let Paduans say: These are of thee.

The sea obeys... (repeat)

To Father, Son, may glory be,
And Holy Ghost eternally.

The sea obeys... (repeat)

V. Pray for us, blessed Anthony:
R. That we may be made worthy of the promises of Christ.

Let us pray:

Let your Church, O God, be made joyful by this solemn commemoration of blessed Anthony, your confessor and doctor; that the Church may always be defended by your spiritual help and merit to possess eternal joys. Through Christ our Lord. Amen.

Prayer to "The Wonder Worker"

After you died, St. Anthony, God chose to make your holiness known to the world and to draw people by working miracles in answer to prayers made in your name. Since then, people have asked God to continue to honor you by working wonders through your intercession. Those who have experienced the power of prayers offered in your name have told how God has answered them.

God has healed the sick,

Restored peace of mind,

Relieved poverty,

And granted favors of all kinds.

Now in this time of need

I ask you, St. Anthony,

To pray with me for the things I desire.

I pray that God may again give us a sign of loving care and providence and that, through you, God may draw us all to the fullness of life and love in eternity.

Amen.

Prayer to Find What Is Lost

St. Anthony, when you prayed your stolen book of prayers was
  given back to you.

Pray now for all of us who have lost things precious and dear.

Pray for all who have lost faith, hope, or the friendship of God.

Pray for us who have lost friends or relatives by death.

Pray for all who have lost peace of mind or spirit.

Pray that we may be given new hope, new faith, new love.

Pray that lost things, needful and helpful to us, may be returned to our keeping.

Or if we must continue in our loss, pray that we may be given Christ's comfort and peace. Amen.

PRAYER TO ST. ANTHONY FOR HELP AND GUIDANCE

Doctor of the Gospel,

light of the holy Church

lover of souls,

true son of Francis of Assisi,

Anthony of Padua,

help us to have a proper devotion to you.

Put into our hearts the flame of love

that we may cherish our merciful Father in heaven.

Teach us to treat our neighbor with Christian charity and forbearance.

May your chastity,

your spirit of prayer,

and your deep inner life

inspire us to be faithful to God above all else.

Accompanied by your prayers may we also be faithful to the vows of our baptism, marriage, or religious life.

May we live with you the gospel of Christ

and grow with you in Him. Amen.

PRAYER OF THANKSGIVING TO ST. ANTHONY

St. Anthony,

father of the poor and comforter of the needy,

I thank you for having come to my aid and consoled me so abundantly.

Help me now to grow in love of our merciful Father
so that, as you said,
the King of Kings may reign in my heart and purify it.
May I live with you the gospel of Christ
and grow with you in Him, who is the Lord. Amen.

Meditations on the Sermons of St. Anthony

Some advice before you begin:
This second part of our novena to St. Anthony is presented as an option. You may not always have time to extend the novena in this way. Or you may prefer to save the meditations for special occasions. It is an option, however, that you will not find in other novenas to St. Anthony. It was designed especially for this book and is based on *St. Anthony of Padua: Wisdom for Today* by Pat McCloskey, O.F.M.

How to use these meditations:
On each of the nine days of your novena, after you have recited the responsory and prayers, reflect on the sermon passage from St. Anthony for that day. Put yourself in a reflective state of mind and heart. Take a deep breath or two, if that helps. Then, through Anthony's intercession, ask the Holy Spirit to help you find a closer union with God as you ponder the sermon passage of St. Anthony as well as the reflection that follows it. Take as much time as you like. Let the Spirit lead you to any further personal meditations of your own. Also feel free to express your personal novena intentions before God and your special friend, St. Anthony of Padua.

Day One: *Embrace the Light of Christ*
St. Anthony: "When it is dark, we do not see how dusty and dirty our house is. Only when the place is flooded with sunlight do we realize its awful condition. So we need the light of God's grace to

show us the real state of our soul and induce us to clean up our hearts!"

Reflection: In John 8:12, Jesus says, "I am the light of the world. Whoever follows me will never walk in darkness but will have the light of life." This first day of our novena is a good time to take stock of how closely we do—or do not—measure up to Christ, our shining model in all things. How does the quality of our love and service to God and humanity compare to that of Christ, our light? But Jesus' light is not only a ray of light that exposes our darkness and shortcomings or puts us in touch with our guilt. It is also a warm flood of comforting sunlight that replaces our darkness and wraps us in God's healing love—a love that gives us a fresh start, lightens our step, and sets us on a new path of Christian service. (Take time for your own reflection. Then close by saying the Prayer of Thanksgiving, p. 103.)

Day Two: *Love Wholly and Not Partially*

St. Anthony: "You shall love the Lord your God with your whole heart. Notice that Christ says: Your whole heart. He doesn't say: Leave a corner of your heart for yourself. He bought the whole of you by giving his whole self for you, that he alone might possess every part of you. Do not try to hold back any part of yourself.... If you really wish to have the whole, then give it all to him, and he will give you all of himself."

Reflection: In chapter six we saw how Anthony was amazed at the mystery of the Incarnation, at how "the Lord of the Universe was wrapped in swaddling clothes" and lying in a "narrow manger." Yes, like St. Francis, Anthony was astonished at God's total gift of self—at how God had stripped himself of glory and entered this world as a helpless child. God held nothing back from us. We see the same intensity of love in God's total self-gift on the cross and as he offers himself to us each day in the Eucharist: "This is my body, which is given for you" (Luke 22:19). Although you and I are simple vessels of clay, we try—with the help of God's mighty Spirit—to respond to God's total gift of Self as *wholeheartedly* as we can. (Take time for your own reflection. Then close by saying the Prayer of Thanksgiving, p. 103.)

Day Three: *Be Careful of Greed*

St. Anthony: "The avaricious man is really not rich, but poor. He does not control his money, but is controlled by it. He does not possess his wealth, but is possessed by it. He may have many things, yet for him he has all too little."

Reflection: It is not wrong to own a car, to provide a house for our family, to take a vacation and enjoy the world God has created. But each of us may need to ask what the desire for money or the amassing of material possessions is doing to the priorities of our lives. Are they giving us greater freedom and energy to serve God and neighbor, or are they making us more selfish and self-absorbed? The book of Proverbs tells us, "Better is a little with the fear of the LORD / than great treasure and trouble with it" (15:16). A good antidote to greed is a spirit of humble gratitude toward God and generosity toward our neighbor. (Take time for your own reflection. Then close with the Prayer of Thanksgiving, p. 103.)

Day Four: *Seek the Face of God Before All Else*

St. Anthony: "Nothing apart from God can satisfy the human heart, which is truly in search of God."

Reflection: As an Augustinian monk for several years, Anthony would have surely been aware of one of the most famous quotations of St. Augustine, which is found near the beginning of his *Confessions:* "You have created us for yourself, O God, and our hearts are restless until they rest in thee." Anthony's brief words above are making the same point. We saw in chapter seven of this book that

St. Anthony never abandoned his contemplative yearning to seek the face of God before all else. Take a moment to get in touch with your heart's inmost desire to be united and at rest with God. Ask Anthony to intercede for you before God that you, like Anthony, may find your own contemplative gift and, indeed, full union with God. (Take time for your own reflection. Close with the Prayer of Thanksgiving, p. 103.)

Day Five: *See Christ in Those Who Suffer*

St. Anthony: "Today Christ stands at the door and knocks in the person of his poor. It is to him that we open when we give aid, when we give ourselves to those in need. For he tells us plainly, 'Just as you did it to one of the least of these who are members of my family, you did it to me' (Matthew 25:40)."

Reflection: Just as we, in this novena, come before St. Anthony and our gracious God to have some need fulfilled, so also may our brothers or sisters come to us with needs and sorrows that we can help alleviate. It is not only through contemplation and prayer that we see the face of Christ but also by showing compassion to the poor and attending to their needs—by comforting a suffering coworker, visiting a sick friend in the hospital, or donating money or our talents to a good cause. St. Anthony found the face of God not only in times of quiet prayer but also by serving those in need. Are we doing the same? (Take time for your own reflection. Close with the Prayer of Thanksgiving, p. 103.)

Day Six: *Let God's Light Shine Through You*

St. Anthony: "When a crystal is touched or struck by the rays of the sun, it gives forth brilliant sparks of light. When the man of faith is touched by the light of God's grace, he too must shine with his good words and deeds, and so bring God's light to others."

Reflection: We know that a glowing piece of crystal is a marvelous thing to see, but it is not the source of its own light. It reflects the sun. As people of faith, we know that God wants us to be instruments of his light and goodness to the world. To be effective transmitters of God's light to others, however, we need first to welcome the light of Christ into our hearts through humble prayer and contemplation, through familiarity with sacred Scripture, through the Eucharist, through serving Christ in the poor, and so forth. Once God's light finds its way into our hearts, we can beam that light to others. (Take time for your own reflection. Close with the Prayer of Thanksgiving, p. 103.)

Day Seven: *See the Depth of Christ's Love*

St. Anthony: "During the meal, Jesus took bread, blessed it and broke it as a sign that his body would be broken, too, through his freely accepted death. The humanity of Christ is like the grape because it was crushed in the winepress of the cross so that his blood flowed forth over all the earth…. 'This is my blood of the new covenant, which shall be shed for many unto the forgiveness of sins.' How great is the charity of the beloved! How great the love of the Bridegroom for his spouse, the Church!"

Reflection: In the Eucharist, Anthony gets a glimpse of the immense love of Christ for each human being, including himself. It is as if Anthony has experienced within himself the full force of Jesus' words: "No one has greater love than this, to lay down one's life for one's friends" (John 15:13). Christ's love for the people of God, Anthony tells us, is like the love of a bridegroom for his bride. Let Anthony's words help you see with renewed faith what the Eucharist teaches us about God's forgiveness and unconditional love for each of us. If you and I understood as clearly as St. Anthony the depth of Christ's love for each of us, surely our love for Christ would grow much stronger. (Take time for your own reflection. Close with the Prayer of Thanksgiving, p. 103.)

Day Eight: *Stay United With Your Healer*

St. Anthony: "No one is closer to us than he who healed our wounds. For the Head is one with his members. Let us therefore love him as our Lord and God."

Reflection: Jesus himself gave us a similar example of the intimate union he shares with us when he gave us the image of the vine and the branches. "I am the vine, you are the branches," Jesus tells us (see John 15:1–10). A branch shares the same vital, nourishing sap that gives life to the vine and brings forth fruit. What a picture of closeness and intimate collaboration! Jesus clearly wants to enjoy and promote this kind of union. "Abide in me as I abide in you," he says. "Those who abide in me and I in them bear much fruit, because apart from me you can do nothing." Anthony's reminder that Christ, who is so close to us and is also our *healer*, makes us value all the more the loving union we share. May Anthony help us never to lose this wonderful awareness of our oneness with Christ. (Take time for your own reflection. Close with the Prayer of Thanksgiving, p. 103.)

Day Nine: *May Christ Deepen Our Love*

St. Anthony: "We beg you, Lord Jesus, bind us with the love of you and our neighbor so that we can love you deeply with our whole heart, and not be separated from you."

Reflection: Just as Anthony often ended his sermons with a prayer, we also end this novena with a prayerful plea to Jesus that we remain in his love. We know that without God's gracious help and without the vine, we, the branches, can produce no fruit. By the very act of praying to God for help, therefore, and seeking Anthony's intercession, we recognize our own dependence on God and our need for support from brothers and sisters in the communion of saints. We also ask our gracious God—through Anthony—to grant us the special intentions of our novena. All that remains is to express our thanks to God, our helper, and to Anthony, our intercessor. On the last day of our novena, we do this again by saying our concluding Prayer of Thanksgiving.

PRAYER OF THANKSGIVING

St. Anthony, God has helped me abundantly
through your prayer and has strengthened me
in my time of need. I thank God and I thank you.
Accept this prayer and my special resolve,
which I now renew, to live always in the love
of Jesus and of my neighbor. Continue to shield me
with your protection and pray to God for the final grace of one day
entering the kingdom of heaven to sing with you
the everlasting mercies of God. Amen.

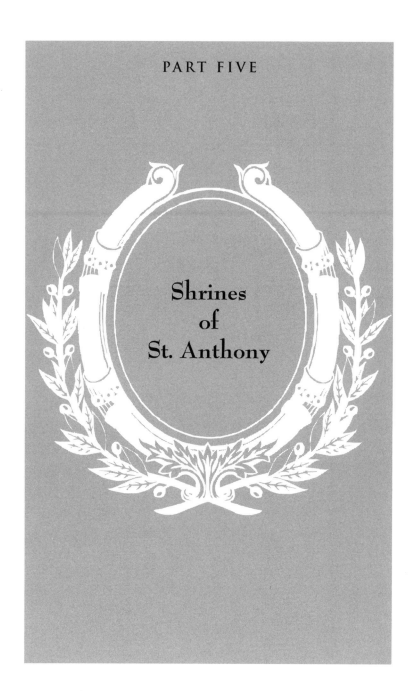

PART FIVE

Shrines
of
St. Anthony

The National Shrine of St. Anthony and Other National and Regional Shrines of St. Anthony

Franciscan Friars, 5000 Colerain Avenue, Cincinnati, Ohio 45223
(513-541-2146). Website: www.StAnthony.org

High on a wooded hill, an easy fifteen-minute drive from downtown Cincinnati, sits St. Anthony Shrine and Friary, whose founding goes back to 1888. The shrine with its quaint chapel has become an oasis for hundreds of visitors who go there each week to find a quiet place to pray, to make the popular Tuesday novenas to St. Anthony, or to attend daily or Sunday Mass. As at many St. Anthony shrines around the world, the annual celebration of the Feast of St. Anthony on June 13 draws the largest crowds of all. So does the solemn novena of nine Tuesdays preceding it.

Since March of 1920, devotees of St. Anthony have been submitting prayer requests to the Cincinnati shrine through *St. Anthony Messenger* magazine. The National Shrine of St. Anthony and the *St. Anthony Messenger* are both operated by the same group of Franciscan friars, the Cincinnati-based Province of St. John the Baptist. For decades, the prayer requests or petitions sent to St. Anthony Messenger Press from around the country (sometimes accompanied by voluntary contributions known as St. Anthony bread) have been carried each week to the national shrine and placed near Anthony's image.

ST. ANTHONY ON THE WEB

Devotees of St. Anthony around the world—or anyone with needs—are able to post their prayer requests online via the website www.StAnthony.org with the comforting awareness that a vast, international online community of petitioners are praying along with them.

In addition to inviting the public to post their prayer requests online, the website provides other interesting features and information regarding the Cincinnati shrine such as a history of the shrine, photos of the shrine, a short life of St. Anthony, e-cards, Mass and novena schedules and more. Visitors to the website can even take a virtual photographic tour of the shrine, as well as its chapel and the lovely grounds surrounding it.

HISTORY OF THE NATIONAL SHRINE

The National Shrine of St. Anthony owes its beginning in 1888 to two generous parishioners who attended the Franciscan-run church of St. Francis Seraph in downtown Cincinnati, Joseph and Elizabeth Nurre. In 1887 the devout couple bought what was then a country estate high above Cincinnati for $18,000 and gave it to the Franciscan friars.

The Nurres also promised to build a Franciscan monastery or friary that would serve as a Franciscan novitiate and as a residence for infirm friars, as well as a refuge for others wishing to make a spiritual retreat. Mt. Airy is the name of the geographic area of Cincinnati where the original estate was located. To this date the friars and their friends still popularly refer to St. Anthony Chapel and Friary as "Mt. Airy."

FROM MONASTERY CHAPEL TO SHRINE

Though the Mt. Airy Chapel was not originally designed or built as a shrine, as mentioned earlier, it wasn't long before people began to make private pilgrimages to this monastery chapel. They would come to spend time in prayer, to attend Mass or to walk the grounds—or perhaps to light a candle before St. Anthony's statue and ask Anthony's intercession for some special need, or even to make a novena. As the number of visitors increased, the chapel began to become known as St. Anthony's Shrine.

The June 1929 issue of *St. Anthony Messenger* seems to be the first issue of the national magazine that actually used the word *shrine* to describe the monastery chapel or to openly publicize the schedule of novenas taking place there. The word *shrine* first appeared on the magazine's June 1929 table of contents page, referring to the chapel as the "saint's shrine." On the same page appeared the notice: "Burn a light at St. Anthony's Shrine in Mount Airy, Ohio.... A light will burn for seven days for one dollar."

The previous year (1928) a small group of friends had met at St. Anthony's friary at the invitation of the friars to establish what is now known as the St. Anthony Shrine Society. The group was formed to help foster devotion to St. Anthony and maintain the shrine. The Shrine Society deserves immense credit for its generous service and for the many improvements it helped to bring about over the years—many of which are still visible today at the shrine or on the surrounding grounds.

Maybe someday you will visit the National Shrine of St. Anthony at Mt. Airy—or at least visit its website at www.StAnthony.org. All are most welcome! If you are unable to visit but would like to see beautiful pictures of it, the 1994 edition of *Catholic Shrines and Places of Pilgrimage in the United States*, published by the United States Catholic Conference in Washington, D.C., features the shrine.

OTHER NATIONAL AND REGIONAL SHRINES OF ST. ANTHONY

St. Anthony Shrine at St. Francis Church, New York City

The major shrine of St. Anthony at St. Francis Church is located in the upper church on the right-hand side, containing an effigy of St. Anthony that is flanked by mosaics of important events in his life. St. Anthony devotions are held on Tuesdays. A nine-week novena precedes the feast of Christmas, and a thirteen-week novena precedes the memorial of St. Anthony (June 13).

St. Francis Church
Franciscan Friars
135 West 31st St.
New York, NY 10001-3202
Telephone: 212-736-8500
Website: www.stfrancisnyc.org
E-mail: info@stfrancisnyc.org

Shrine Church of St. Anthony, New York City

Devotions to St. Anthony are held on Tuesdays in this church dedicated to St. Anthony of Padua and under the care of the Franciscan friars. A thirteen-week novena precedes the memorial of St. Anthony.

St. Anthony of Padua Church
Franciscan Friars
154 Sullivan St.
New York, NY 10012
Telephone: 212-777-2755
Website: www.stanthonynyc.org
E-mail: stanthonychurch@aol.com

St. Anthony Shrine at Graymoor, Garrison, New York

This large outdoor shrine is located on the beautiful grounds of the Franciscan Friars of the Atonement at Graymoor, near Garrison, New York. The shrine is a popular pilgrimage destination before and after the annual memorial day and throughout the year. There is a bookstore on the grounds.

Graymoor
1350 Route 9, PO Box 300
Garrison, NY 10524-0301
Telephone: 845-424-3671
Website: www.atonementfriars.org
E-mail: info@atonementfriars.org

St. Anthony Shrine, Arch Street, Boston, Massachusetts

This shrine, also known as the "Church on Arch Street," is run by the Franciscan friars. Many friends of St. Anthony come to his shrine in the lower-level church for quiet reflection or to seek Anthony's intercession—or to visit the other shrines nearby. Devotions to St. Anthony are held on Tuesdays. A nine-week novena precedes Christmas, and a thirteen-week novena precedes the memorial of St. Anthony.

St. Anthony Shrine
Franciscan Friars
100 Arch St.
Boston, MA 02110
Telephone: 617-542-6440
Website: www.saintanthonyshrine.org
E-mail: info@stanthonyshrine.org

Shrine of St. Anthony, Paterson, New Jersey

This St. Anthony Shrine is located at St. Bonaventure Church and is also operated by the Franciscan friars. Devotions to St. Anthony are held on Tuesdays. A nine-week novena precedes the feast of Christmas, and a thirteen-week novena precedes the memorial of St. Anthony.

St. Anthony Shrine
Franciscan Friars
St. Bonaventure Church
174 Ramsey St.
Paterson, NJ 07501-3215
Telephone: 973-279-1016
Website: www.stbonspaterson.org
E-mail: office@stbonspaterson.org

Shrine of St. Anthony, Ellicott City, Maryland

The shrine—the home of a major relic of St. Anthony—is administered by the conventual Franciscan friars. It is open daily for private and group visits. The shrine is also the home of the "The Companions of St. Anthony." There is a bookstore on site.

Shrine of St. Anthony
Franciscan Friars
12290 Folly Quarter Rd.
Ellicott City, MD 21042
Telephone: 410-531-2800
Website: www.shrineofstanthony.org
E-mail: info@shrineofstanthony.org

Shrine of St. Anthony at the Franciscan Monastery, Washington, D.C.

Replicas of the Holy Land shrines are a big attraction at the monastery, but many visitors pray daily and leave petitions at the altar of St. Anthony in the monastery church. St. Anthony devotions are held on Tuesdays, and a nine-week novena precedes the memorial of St. Anthony. There is a bookstore on site.

Franciscan Monastery of the Holy Land
Franciscan Friars of the Holy Land

1400 Quincy St., NE
Washington, DC 20017
Telephone: 202-526-6800
Website: www.myfranciscan.org
E-mail: mail@myfranciscan.org

The Shrine of St. Anthony at St. Peter's Church, Chicago, Illinois
The shrine, located inside St. Peter's Church in the heart of the
Loop, Chicago's downtown area, attracts hundreds of visitors each
day. After from the Eucharist and the sacrament of reconciliation,
St. Anthony devotions at St. Peter's draw the largest crowds. There
is a bookstore on site.

St. Peter's Church in the Loop
Franciscan Friars
110 West Madison St.
Chicago, IL 60602-4196
Telephone: 312-372-5111
Website: www.stpetersloop.org
E-mail:stpeterloop@aol.com

St. Anthony's Chapel, Pittsburgh, Pennsylvania (Troy Hill)
This devotional chapel is administered by nearby Most Holy Name
of Jesus Parish. Construction began on the chapel in 1880 under
the direction of Fr. Suitbert Mollinger, who was also first pastor
of the parish church. The chapel was dedicated on the feast of St.
Anthony, June 13, 1883. A popular St. Anthony shrine, the chapel
also houses Fr. Mollinger's extensive collection of relics. St. Anthony
novenas are held on Tuesdays, and a thirteen-week novena precedes
the memorial of St. Anthony. The chapel is open Tuesday, Thursday,
Saturday, and Sunday (1:00 to 4:00 P.M.). There is a religious gift
shop on site, including a selection of books and pamphlets.

St. Anthony Chapel
1704 Harpster St.
Pittsburgh, PA 15212
Telephone: 412-231-2994
Website: www.saintanthonyschapel.org

About the Authors

Leonard Foley, O.F.M. (1913–1994), was a writer of popular articles for *St. Anthony Messenger* for over fifty years, as well as its editor from 1964 to 1966. Among his many books are the bestsellers *Believing in Jesus* and *Saint of the Day*. A popular preacher and lecturer, Fr. Leonard was especially adept at communicating the themes and spirit of Vatican II with insight, wit, and the language of the day.

Norman Perry, O.F.M. (1929–1999), was associate editor of *St. Anthony Messenger* from 1966 to 1981 and then its editor-in-chief for eighteen years. In 1997, Fr. Norman received the highest award of the Catholic Press Association, the St. Francis de Sales Award for lifetime achievement. Before his work in journalism he was a teacher in Franciscan high schools and, like St. Anthony himself, a roving preacher of popular missions and retreats.

Carol Ann Morrow was a staff member of *St. Anthony Messenger* from 1985 to her retirement in 2007. She wrote *A Retreat With Anthony of Padua: Finding Our Way* (St. Anthony Messenger Press), which was inspired by her pilgrimages to Portugal and Italy in the footsteps of Sts. Francis and Anthony. She is the author of *Forgiving Is Smart for Your Heart*.

Jack Wintz, O.F.M., has been an editor, writer, and photographer at *St. Anthony Messenger* since 1972 and served as editor-in-chief from 1999 to 2002. He has been editor of *Catholic Update* since 1973. He is the author of *Friar Jack's E-Spirations* and *Will I See My Dog in Heaven?* He has prayed at St. Anthony's tomb in Padua and has made several trips to Assisi, Italy—and to many other countries—over the years.